LIVING AROUND THE NOW CHILD

DAN H. WOODWARD
Black Hawk Area Special Education District
Moline, Illinois

NORMA BIONDO
Community Mental Health Center of Scott County
Davenport, Iowa

LIVING AROUND THE NOW CHILD

CHARLES E. MERRILL PUBLISHING COMPANY
A Bell & Howell Company
Columbus, Ohio

THE SLOW LEARNER SERIES

edited by Newell C. Kephart, Ph.D.

International Standard Book Number: 0-675-09109-8 *casebound*
0-675-09108-x *paperback*

Library of Congress Catalog Card Number: 72-075052

1   2   3   4   5   6   7   8   9   10   —   76   75   74   73   72

Printed in the United States of America

Foreword

The child with learning disability is a "different" child. His behavior is unpredictable. His responses are bizarre and often uninterpretable. His likes and dislikes seem completely random. One never knows what he is going to do and even he does not often know why he did it. He is an enigma to his teacher, a riddle to his peers and a puzzle to his parents. Most of all he is a source of continual frustration to himself for he can never predict with certainty how his actions are going to come out.

Professionals in schools and clinics who have been forced to deal directly with the difficult learning problems of these children have become aware of the nature of their difficulties. We have invented technical terms and identified symptomatology which will permit us to talk to each other about them. We have not, however, reduced this technical jargon to everyday behavior occurrences so that our language is intelligible to other people. As a result many classroom teachers see the same behavior we see but cannot connect what they see with our polysyllabic language. Therefore, despite our rhetoric, they do not really understand the child's problem nor can they interpret his bizarre behavior.

The present volume attempts to describe learning disabilities in terms of common behavior manifestations which can be seen in any classroom. These behaviors are interpreted in terms of logical explanations based on describable, even though not completely empirically established, methods of processing data used by the child. Taken together they represent an operational definition of learning disability. Using such descriptive definitions, the teacher can at least recognize some of the behaviors she sees as evidence of learning problems and can hypothesize an explanation for the child's seemingly unintelligible acts. Instead of blaming these behaviors on stupidity, orneriness or lack of motivation, she can interpret them for what they are.

Great as is the quandary of the teacher, that of the parent is even greater. Too often, the parent is the most forgotten element in the entire complex. We forget that he has the same problems we have but he has them in greatly magnified intensity. Whereas we have this child for a few hours a day in a limited and controlled situation, he has him twenty-four hours in all kinds of situations and all types of demands. He sees the same bizarre behaviors we see but he sees them over time and in an infinite variety of manifestations.

One of the most neglected areas in learning disability is that of parent counseling. The technical terms and ill-defined symptoms which are so difficult for us are frequently pure gibberish to him. Furthermore, one clinician will use one set of these terms and another clinician, talking about the same problem, uses a completely different set of language. It is no wonder the parent is confused. In all this talk, nobody has mentioned the everyday behaviors which are giving this parent so much distress. The present authors talk to parents in their own language about their own problems.

Much valuable information can be gained from parents and much valuable aid in the child's handling can be obtained from them if one can only learn to communicate. The experiences of agencies, such as the Glen Haven Achievement Center, which deliberately make use of parent assistance, are proof of the usefulness of the parent in caring for the needs of his own child. When a parent understands the problem, he need no longer be afraid of a technical term, he can attack his own problem. He need no longer be frustrated by unrecognizable behavior, he can intelligently alter that behavior. He need no longer frustrate the child by simple but, for him, impossible demands. He can aid the child in the achievement of increasingly complex accomplishments. He need no longer blame the school for the child's lack of academic progress; he can help in the teaching function.

Among the many aspects of learning disability covered by the authors, one needs special comments because of its close connection with the child's everyday acts. This child lacks a sense of time. There is no yesterday or tomorrow, there is only today. Each act stands on its own, dictated by its own stimuli and has little to do with what went before or what may come after. It is this independence of the individual act which makes the child so impulsive, so seemingly unappreciative, so forgetful and so unpredictable. Punishment has little effect because it occurs after the fact and the fact has already passed into oblivion.

To understand this simple fact is to go far toward understanding the child and especially toward permitting an interpretation of his behavior to those who must deal with his unique actions in day to day situations. It is felt that the present volume can greatly aid in the understanding of the child with learning disabilities as he functions in everyday life and to alert us to the necessity of interpreting these idiosyncracies to those who must deal with him on a daily basis. The school or the clinic cannot solve his problems alone. They must depend on the aid of the parent and all whose contacts with the child are prolonged and involve major consequences to his welfare.

Newell C. Kephart
Glen Haven Achievement Center
Fort Collins, Colorado

Preface

This book is about children referred to school psychologists and mental health centers; children with problems labeled "emotional," "behavioral," and "perceptual." Almost always they are said to be "underachievers."

It is written for those in all disciplines who work with children and with these children's parents. Parents presently bear an unreasonable burden of blame.

These children have always been with us. You know several for their number is estimated at two out of ten. Their difficulty is not an obvious one for they bear no immediately recognizable stigmata. They have been variously labeled and variously explained, usually in terms of classroom behavior and remediation procedures.

This book is about the total child—at home and at school; the feelings and attitudes his mystery fosters in both parents and teachers; and the negative labels that prevent change.

This child is different and his differentness stems from his existence in a different time dimension, from his lack of ulterior motives—not from devils or badness inside him, and not from any "unconscious" destructive motives on the part of his parents.

Dan Woodward
Norma Biondo

Acknowledgments

We wish primarily to acknowledge the cooperation of many parents, their children, and the children's teachers—most gratefully those who suffered through our early ignorance. There is no substitute for direct experience in understanding children with problems, and this direct experience was possible through our association with the Community Mental Health Center of Scott County in Davenport, Iowa, and the Black Hawk Area Special Education District in Moline, Illinois.

Dr. Newell Kephart's patient encouragement kept us going during periods of doubt and we wish to acknowledge the very practical suggestions of our friend Donald Swanson. Chrystyne Cotting edited and pink-slipped the manuscript into a book with intelligence, tolerance and warmth.

Special thanks goes to those whose resistance, opposition, and misconceptions made us determined to write this book and forced us to be more clear in our formulations. Our children, Vitina and Ax, deserve mention. Their refusal to tolerate neglect gracefully kept us focused on our primary task of being their parents.

D. W.
N. B.

Dedicated to our friend

RUTHIE SWANSON

who

lives and loves doing

Contents

LIVING AROUND THE NOW CHILD

"It's not so bad, Stan. The Doctor says we're a borderline case."

part 1

Help! !

"It's bad . . . nobody knows *how* bad.
It doesn't seem to be getting that much better.
When will it end? Where will it end?
If he's like this now, what will he be when he's 18?
We've tried everything and nothing works.
He's different. He's really different!
Can it change?
Can *he* change?
He's in complete control. He has things the way he wants them.
He really isn't hurting very much. We are.
Can he change?
Can he learn?—Not reading or arithmetic . . . we don't mean that.
But . . . how it is with him.—To understand that there *is* a consequence—that there *is* a tomorrow.
He is so irresponsible!!"

*"Seventeen professionals
in two weeks
haven't been able to
figure out this kid who
doesn't weigh forty pounds
sopping wet and he sits
there looking like he
hasn't done a thing."*

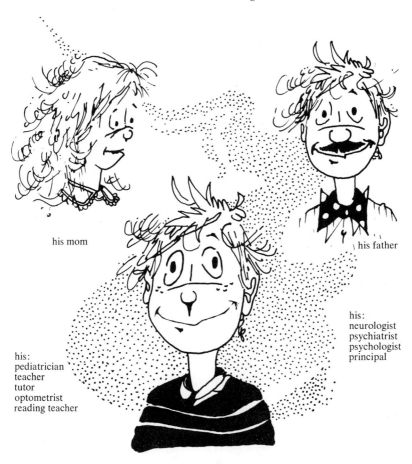

his mom

his father

his:
pediatrician
teacher
tutor
optometrist
reading teacher

his:
neurologist
psychiatrist
psychologist
principal

"The poor kid—he doesn't get enough attention!!"

String for the Beads

A mental health center setting provides some unique advantages in obtaining a more global view of childrens' functioning in relation to both family and school. There is more intimate contact with parents than in most schools. The mental health worker is able to explore family interaction in more detail. We explore with the child more freely because we are not assigned the task of instilling a prescribed body of knowledge, as is the teacher.

Our focus is on those particular children referred to the mental health center—usually, but not always, by schools—who underachieve in one subject or another and who often exhibit problems in behavioral control. Of particular interest is the large group of children—mostly boys (the ratio of referrals is eight boys to one girl)—variously described as having visual-motor problems, as being hyperactive, dyslexic, or with poor impulse control—who usually have an "emotional overlay" of one sort or another.

The characteristics displayed in the learning situation are described separately from those in social situations and separate prescriptions are written for each piece of the child.

Our contacts with parents, teachers, and children lead us to believe the same basic factors account for the child's difficulty in functioning both at home and at school. The same difficulty in remembering timestables may make remembering to carry out the trash difficult—and, indeed, both behaviors may be labeled "irresponsible" or "not caring" and labels tend to compound the problems.

This book is written to attempt some connections between behavior at school and behavior at home, to present possibilities for a new point of view. It's a book about observations and consequent attitudes—it deals with the whole child, mostly with his unarticulated point of view. Seeing problems from the child's point of view untangles some puzzles, relieves some guilt, and allows an approach based on understanding, not blame.

This isn't a book of prescriptions for remediation of school subjects, of visual-motor training, gross-motor coordination, or any of the rest.

This book is about providing a climate which permits these children to grow as parents and teachers provide opportunities and management based on what is, and not on what ought to be.

Dear Teacher:

This child is no stranger to you. You've had him in class. He's the one who:

- —doesn't fit
- —takes most of your time
- —learns—but not what you teach
- —raises his hand wanting to know what to do, right after you've given instructions
- —just sits and stares when you tell him to get busy
- —does OK if you stand beside him or work with him alone
- —quits if it looks like he's going to have trouble
- —goes wild during "free-time"
- —is so helpful he's a nuisance
- —will do anything you ask, as long as it isn't schoolwork
- —answers out of turn
- —talks so bright, but can't write a simple sentence
- —doesn't know what to do next
- —becomes the class clown
- —rushes through his work
- —makes you feel like a failure
- —never finishes an assignment
- —can't sit still
- —has to know everything that's going on
- —can't keep his hands to himself
- —loses his place
- —hollers "Wait-wait!" when you're dictating spelling words
- —needs a recess every half hour
- —is not working up to capacity
- —always has to be first
- —never admits he does anything wrong
- —has the messiest desk
- —could do better if he wanted to
- —calls you at home for assignments
- —loses the messages you send home, or leaves them in his pockets
- —makes you wonder if you really want to come back tomorrow

Your job would be so much easier if he were not there. You've tried everything and nothing works. He doesn't learn what you try to teach him. He makes you question your own competence. That's bad enough, but he also interferes with your efforts to teach the others in the class. He spoils it for them. You've tried—you've done your best—but somehow it wasn't good enough. Maybe he should be transferred to a special education class—somewhere—anywhere.

"He goes, or I go."
"He isn't stupid, I can see that."
"He knows a lot of things."
"He learns, but I don't know *how* he learns."
"He should be able to do the work, but he doesn't do it."
"I can't figure him out."

This Child Is Different

He does not fit the social system. He does not fit the school system and has difficulty meshing with family expectations. This child is a puzzle. We focus on what's wrong with *him* that he doesn't fit our systems, and then we focus on what's wrong with our systems that they are too narrow to include him. This child becomes "these children" as they appear in increasing numbers. Current estimates number them at two out of every ten children! The systems offer many explanations:

the school suspects a "poor home situation"
the family concludes that he "got off to a poor start in school"
he doesn't get enough love at home
he gets too much love at home
the first-grade teacher was too strict
the first-grade teacher was too lenient

As the child gets older he becomes more acceptable as a target. He doesn't say much so it is easier to impose our definitions on him:

he doesn't care
he could if he tried
he doesn't want to be successful
he is irresponsible

And after awhile, he accepts our definitions as his own and becomes defensive—as does the school—as do the parents—and deciding who is wrong substitutes for any really effective looking and working together.

We professionals call him names:
hyperkinetic impulse disorder
maturational lag
neurologic imbalance
learning disability
perceptually handicapped
hyperactive child

(there are at least 33 more)

. . . and different professionals call him different names . . . and we decide that the problem is due to "poor inter-professional communication." We have interdisciplinary meetings and decide that we'll all call him the same name. We talk about the "organism." We talk about "the motor system." We talk about "the sensory system." We talk about "the perceptual system." We get so interested in the fragments we forget that we are fragmenting this child whom we describe as fragmented. We sail into the abstract, never-never land of technicalities and long words. We find people and systems to blame, and we use blame as the bucket to hold all our beads because we have no cord to string them on.

the kid as seen by his neurologist

the optometrist's view

the audiologist's view

the speech therapist's view

the psychologist's view

the psychiatrist's view

the kid's point of view

Meanwhile, back at the ranch, this child is getting older and his parents are getting to look like Grant Wood paintings and his teacher is keeping the red-pencil industry working three shifts.

The child wants to do better, the parents want him to do better and the teacher would be mightily pleased to be able to *help* him to do better. They are immobilized by mutual defensiveness, contradictory recommendations, and they are trapped in their systems. It would help if everyone could get on the same side, agree on a point of view, and then try some things.

This book makes use of the observations made by parents and teachers of "these children" as well as the behavior and observations of "the child" himself. They live together and this records the comic and the tragic in their attempts to assist the child to be more liveable and lovable. They are doing the job now and want to do it better.

Mom

"I'm on top of things."

Parents Say

Parents live with the child. They make observations. We listen to what they share with us:

We've tried everything and nothing works.

I guess it's our fault, but we don't know what we're doing wrong.

It's different with our other children.

Evenings are the worst.

Living with him is like walking on eggs.

If he's this way now, what will he be by the time he's 18?

I get so angry that I'm ashamed of myself.

I do more for him than any of my children, and it's never enough.

He doesn't seem to appreciate anything.

There are times when I give in to him just to keep the peace.

When I want him to look his best, he acts the worst—like in church or at the grocery store.

He embarrasses us.

We accuse each other. I tell my husband he's a terrible father; he tells me I'm a lousy mother.

I know he must be emotionally disturbed. Is it my fault?

No one knows better than we that he is upset. And things *have* happened that *would* upset him. He was only 11 months old when has brother was born. Last year his older brother got diabetes; maybe we didn't give him enough attention.

His brother and sister throw him out of the room if he becomes too much of a pest at home.

I guess we can handle him at home, but we can't go to school with him.

He can't sit still. He's on the move constantly. He needs a lot of space.

If I have him by myself, it's not so bad. But he won't share me with anyone.

He forgives so easily—I'm still mad and he's puckered up wanting a kiss.

He's got a hair-trigger temper; he's the neighborhood bully.

He can't read and he's got an I.Q. of 124.

Most of the time he acts like he just doesn't care.

You can never tell what might set him off; it can be the least little thing. It's like poking a balloon that's filled to the limit; one little prick and it goes to pieces.

I don't understand . . . sometimes he can be so *good*.

He got off to a bad start in school. We figured he didn't have a good first-grade teacher.

I make him study every night.

I'm tired of taking the fifth grade all over again.

When he leaves home he knows every spelling word perfectly, and then he misses seven on the test.

He can't play by himself. He has a basement full of toys but he doesn't know what to do.

One Sunday after church he asked, "Well, Dad, what are you going to do with me today?"

He takes up all my time.

They say he needs more attention; he gets more than any of the other kids get.

I have to watch him all the time.

If I keep him busy doing something it's better.

He was all right until he started to school. It must be their fault.

I get disgusted with him, but not nearly as disgusted as he gets with himself.

They say he doesn't try, but at some things he works till he drops.

It's hard for him to get started.

You should see the way he shovels the snow off the walks; it's beautiful.

Most of the time he never remembers his chores. I have to remind him constantly. It's easier to do it myself.

He forgets what I send him after.

He thinks only of himself.

He never wears out . . . he's never tired. He goes all day and then he's the first one up in the morning.

He never stops talking.

He whispers directions to himself all the time.

He's either a complete mess or he's perfect.

There's no in-between; he's all or nothing.

You should see the way he keeps his clothes in his drawers; if one pair of socks gets out of place, he blows up.

He's so disorganized! He doesn't know where anything is.

He's got to know everything; he always wants to know, "What's next?"

He doesn't wet the bed away from home. There must be something wrong with us.

"Did you say 'Send him to camp'?!"

At his grandmothers' you couldn't ask for a nicer child.

Last night he prayed to be good.

I thought he was going to try to change, but it didn't last.

He cons me all the time.

He always has to be first.

He's a very poor loser. He's got to win.

We plan a surprise for him and it blows up in our faces.

If something new is going to happen—even if it's nice—we found out you better tell him just before it happens. He can't stand surprises.

I'm worn out. I just get one thing settled and he figures out a new way to bug me.

I go to people for advice. One tells me one thing, another tells me something else. I just get more confused.

It's hard to have someone tell you that you don't love your child.

I have to say I get awfully mad at him sometimes, but I don't hate him.

Sometimes I think he hates himself.

I feel so sorry for him I could cry.

He's not an easy child to live with.

He never finishes anything.

But he's not all bad. There are times when you couldn't ask for a nicer boy.

He's smart enough. He ought to be doing better.

Around others he's not so bad—they think I'm making it up when I tell them how he is at home.

It's not fair to the other children. Sometimes they have to get away from him; sometimes I have to get away from him, too.

He was in psychotherapy for two years in Wisconsin and he's still no better.

Every year it's the same thing. We've had marital counseling. We don't seem to have problems between us any more, but it doesn't seem to make any difference with him.

"He's so unhappy."

Everyone says it's because I'm his stepmother, but believe me, if I didn't sit down on him he wouldn't get anything done.

Here it is the middle of February and every night he insists upon hearing "The Twelve Days of Christmas." It's driving me out of my mind.

If he doesn't get to do what he wants to do, sometimes he'll keep us up half the night.

OK, so he doesn't do so well in school. I can accept that . . . but why can't he be happy?

They say he's above average in intelligence, but here he is in the sixth grade, and he can't even tell time.

He never wants to play with kids his own age; they're either younger or older.

He's so careless . . . he has to do everything fast.

He always says, "I'm sorry," and I believe him at the time, but then he turns right around and does it again.

He hates to go to school in the morning. Sometimes he tells me he has the stomachache.

It's a funny thing. I know he doesn't do well in school, but he seems to like to go.

He brought me this paper he didn't finish at school and I had to sign it and send it back. He felt so ashamed.

I think there is something more important for him to do than school work every night. He has to have time to play.

His sister tells him that she hates him and wishes that he would live somewhere else.

I just don't know what to do to help him.

He'll cheat, lie, anything . . . he has to win.

If only he'd quit screaming, "You hate me."

He makes us look bad as parents.

He's got five brothers and sisters and they're all right. What is it with him?

If he had been my first, he would have been my last.

When I was a kid, we lived on the farm. Maybe that's what he needs.

If he gets out of my sight in a store, he screams. It's like he was afraid that I was going to leave him.

Somebody said he was reacting to my unconscious negative feelings. Believe me, they aren't unconscious!

I'm so tired of going to that school. What do they expect me to do?

Some nights he comes home from school crying, and *they* say he doesn't care.

People think I'm awful because I have him scrub floors and wash windows, but he likes it.

I have to admit I was glad when he started to school.

He's just like his father in so many ways.

His father winds up spanking him, and I wind up crying.

He doesn't seem to have any sense of responsibility.

He never knows what to do next.

He really isn't a bad boy.

If I'm sick and he knows I'm sick, he waits on me hand and foot.

OK, so that's the way he behaved in your office. I wish you could come to supper one night!

One of these days I'm going to make a tape recording so you can hear how bad it really is!

"Sometimes we give in just to keep the peace."

He gets everybody screaming at him.

It's terrible to feel like such a failure as a mother.

I blame *my* mother. She must have done something wrong with me.

He sure is a puzzle. It just doesn't make sense.

I know we shouldn't laugh at him, but sometimes you just can't help it. He's a clown.

The other kids egg him on. But he doesn't know when to stop.

Sometimes I have to bite my tongue to keep from laughing.

He hams up everything. Sometimes it's funny, but sometimes it's not.

In school he gets to be the class clown.

What's going to happen to this boy when he's grown up?

He's like his father, my first husband, the alcoholic.

Isn't there some kind of pill that could quiet him down? Or one that would quiet me down?

Find me some pills and we'll both take 'em.

He's a born loser. But he doesn't know it.

He can't make choices; he can't even make up his mind if he wants a vanilla or chocolate ice cream cone.

I give him a chance to do something nice and he always says "no."

Who's running this family anyway?

I get tired of being pushed around by a little kid.

He wants to hang on me all the time. I give him a kiss to prove that I love him. In the middle of dishes he has to have a kiss.

He's got to be right all the time.

That boy is just like me when I was his age.

He's easily led.

" 'Bye, Mom. Goin' to school now!"

Sure, *you* can get along with him all right, but you only see him an hour a week.

I do so want to be a good mother.

I'm going to work.

If I hadn't had five others, I wouldn't have known he was different.

I don't think there is anything wrong with his personality. He has plenty of that. He has a pretty strong impact on people.

He needs more sleep than most kids.

She has lost three pairs of gloves already this winter.

He uses my tools and leaves them wherever he drops them.

He thinks everybody is his friend.

He waits until the last minute and then comes up with a list of things a yard long that he has to take to school.

He never feels guilty for his mistakes.

He says he is sorry but he doesn't mean it.

Trying to reason with him is pointless.

He loves animals.

We think he should go to camp. It would be good for him to get away from us.

We're open for suggestions.

Teachers Say

When this child starts to school, he becomes the teacher's responsibility. Teachers make observations. This is how it is with them:

He can't sit still.

He answers all the questions. Everytime I ask a question, he has the answer right now, and what's so frustrating is that 99% of the time he's right.

None of the other kids have a chance to answer anything.

He speaks out and it's like he can't help it. He's got to *say*.

He says, "I'll do the assignment," and then he looks out the window, walks around, doesn't do anything.

He can't work on his own.

He's not mean, but he's so *active*.

He grabs someone by the arm or gives a little push to make a point. Not mean, but a nuisance.

He's on the go all the time. He's very energetic.

I'm not complaining . . . he's a nice kid, smart . . . but different.

It helps to give him jobs to do, but if I do it all the time the other kids get jealous.

It's a real problem for a teacher because you're supposed to treat all the kids the same. How can you treat him the same? He's different!

He has to see everything that's going on. So I put him in the back of the room. When he was sitting in the front, he was always turning around, and that got to be a nuisance.

The kids like him a lot, but he can't sit still, he doesn't finish his work and his writing is terrible.

He's in the low math group.

He has a good background of knowledge. Parents haven't overprotected him; they've taken him out.

He has a lot of information and he is interested in many things.

He can talk about many things, but he can't write a simple sentence.

In spite of all the positive things about him, he still is the biggest problem I have.

I know that he could do better in reading if only he would discipline himself.

He loses things. He was getting behind because he was having to erase all the time and he couldn't find his eraser.

He's a very sensitive boy. He can tell how far he can push me. He watches me and keeps an eye on me as much as I keep an eye on him. And he knows when I'll get mad, but even though he knows it he still keeps doing what he's doing.

It's like he was driven to be successful.

Everytime when he messes up he says, "I didn't mean to do that."

If he was the only student in my class he would be a great joy.

One of the reasons his writing is bad is because he goes fast and has to do everything in a hurry. He is careless.

It looks like he doesn't care, but I think he does.

Maybe he cares too much.

He's messy; he's careless.

If only he would take his time . . . but it's like he has to do it fast because he can't stay with it very long.

If he could only settle down.

He needs a recess every half hour.

The afternoons are the worst.

What can I do to help?

There are days when he has me climbing the walls.

When he writes, he runs it all together. You can't tell where one words begins and the other ends.

It's a funny thing . . . when I stand right next to him he can do the work very well. But when I walk away he does nothing.

This child simply cannot function in the second grade and I don't need any test to tell me that!

I've done everything I know with this child; it must be his homelife.

He's jerky in everything he does.

He could do it if he really wanted to.

He simply is not working up to his capacity.

Why don't you transfer him to another room?

He makes me feel like a failure.

I've been teaching for twenty years and I've never had a kid like him.

He doesn't give *me* any trouble . . . I let him do what he wants.

He never completes an assignment.

Is there any possibility of sending him somewhere else?

This is my first year of teaching and probably my last.

There's a limit to what you can take.

When I was learning to be a teacher they didn't say anything in the books about him!

I checked with his last year's teacher. She had the same trouble.

He reacts to the slightest provocation. It doesn't take much to trigger him.

What do I do when he says he *won't* do his work?

He always has to be first.

The other kids don't want to play with him because he never sticks to anything.

If he loses, he changes the rules.

He's so helpful to me, he's a nuisance.

He never admits he's done anything wrong.

He turns everything around so it's someone else's fault.

He denies everything.

He has no sense of responsibility for anything.

Nothing works with him. I know, I've tried everything.

He could do better if he wanted to.

He's eight years old and a big boy!

There are three other kids in that family and there's nothing wrong with them.

What he needs is discipline.

When he has free time on his hands, he's really in trouble. But if I can keep him busy, it doesn't matter what—scrubbing the floor, picking up papers—he's willing to do it and does a good job.

He'll do anything I ask him to do, as long as it's not school work.

I feel sorry for his mother.

If that was my child, I'd kill myself.

The trouble is, I can't get away from him. It would be nice to have a little relief.

I hear he's got a brother.

I let him do what he wants to do and guess what? He got the folding chair and it was too tall for him and I had to listen for fifteen minutes how I should get a folding chair where his feet could reach the floor.

Now he has a new trick; he goes around burping in people's ears. He's always looking for attention.

He's OK if I work with him by himself; otherwise he just goes crazy.

When he fails he breaks down completely.

If it looks like he's going to have trouble, he quits.

Well, maybe it *is* too much to expect him to do reading problems, if he can't read.

You can't kid me . . . that boy can read; he's just putting on.

He likes gruesome stories. He's going to get everybody on his side and kill everybody else . . . especially teachers and parents who nag him.

He says he'd like to be on a deserted island all by himself.

He's a bad kid.

Everyday I say, "Today I'm not going to lose my temper," but I'm lucky if I hold out until noon.

Listen, you transfer this child to another room or I quit. One of us has got to go.

Everyday I say, "Today it's going to be better," and very often for five minutes it is, but it never holds. What does it take to make this boy decent?

So he's got to be special. Well, he gets this new record player for Christmas. It's a special kind, and I think to myself, that will do it. He has something no one else has. You think I'm right? Wrong. Nothing does it. Well, he *is* unique. He's got a hair-trigger temper and he's a bully and he can't read. And with an I.Q. of 132—that's unique!

Well, it's nothing new. He was that way last year.

If he says "Minnesota" one more time, I'll scream!

He's not getting enough love at home.

You should see his desk. The biggest mess you ever saw.

When he holds the pencil, he has a death grip on it . . . pushes the lead through the paper. He must be a very angry boy.

The Child Says

The child tells us how it is with him. It's just like he says—no more.

I'm the dumbest kid in the class.
I'm not good at that.
If you want somebody to draw cars, ask my brother.
Can I shoot some darts *now*?
Do you have any idea where my shoes are?
I've got to do it fast before I lose it.
That's cinchy, man, cinchy.
Sometimes I can do it—sometimes I can't.
Sometimes I make a boo-boo—sometimes I don't.
Sometimes I know I can do it—sometimes I don't think I can.
Sometimes I do it good—sometimes not as good as I think I
    should.
Man, I sure wish I didn't have to do this.
That's haaaaaard!
Sometimes I say it ain't; sometimes I say it is . . . h-a-a-a-rd!
My mother makes me sweep the floor.
What time is it?
How would you like it if you had to get up in the morning
    and sit in one place all day doing arithmetic problems.
That's too hard for me.
That's too easy for me.
One thing I don't like is for others to see me as stupid.
When I was in the fourth and fifth grade I just rushed through;
    I didn't care, and now I can't do it.

26

"The teacher says I'm your fault, Mom."

I miss too many steps in-between.

I have horrible penmanship. I could do better if I wanted to, but I just don't take time.

I dunno—all of a sudden I'm naughty—I don't know why.

I pray every night to be good.

Everyone says I'm smart enough—I don't know why I can't.

I was good in church last Sunday.

How should I know . . . I'm just a little kid.

I like to let my eyes wander and that's how come I see so many things like those door chimes.

You shouldn't ask me to do things like that . . . I'm just a little kid.

I can know my alphabet when I get grown up.

How much longer do I have to stay here?

Other kids don't have this problem. Why is it so hard for me?

How come you're so mad all the time?

I don't have anything to do.

Let's do something.

How much did your desk cost?

Smokin' will make your lungs black and stink.

My teacher says it's your fault, Mom.

What happened?

If the cops kill my boyfriend, I will go to the funeral.

I wish I wasn't born—I think I'm too much trouble to my
    parents.

A Cup of Beads

On a comparative basis, the child has little to say. Some things, however, are obvious:

—He tends to repeat descriptions of himself that he has heard from others.
—He has little confidence in his ability to perform.
—He says little about himself.
—He is direct.
—He does not express negative or positive feelings about others.
—He is concerned about time.

He appears very calm in most instances—quite in contrast to the emotional havoc he has apparently generated in his parents and teachers. He *is* a puzzle. What is the power within him that generates the paradoxical views?

—He's smart enough but he can't find anything.
—He never finishes anything, but sometimes he works until he drops.
—He doesn't care, but he comes home from school crying and feeds homeless dogs.
—He's either a complete mess or he's perfect.
—He needs help, but he doesn't know that he does.
—He's puzzled about himself, but doesn't seem worried.
—When you have him alone, he's no problem, but in a group! ! !
—There are times when you couldn't ask for a nicer boy, but there are other times when he drives you up the wall.

You make observations and try to make sense out of the data; to see the world from the child's point of view. You conclude that he must have a view very different from his parents or his teachers, but he doesn't have the words to tell you. You make guesses and ask questions of the parents and of the teachers and you find the following:

—He lives mostly in the present with little knowledge of the past and little concern about the future.
—He does not respond to innuendoes or subtleties; he is *direct*.
—He says how it is right now and you can believe him.
—He attends to only one aspect of a message and does not respond to the implied.
—The more complex the situation, the less likely will he be to respond appropriately.
—His power is that he has no power—mostly it is his lack of response to ordinary social game playing that is so unnerving.
—He carries one-to-one relationship techniques into the group situation—most often they do not fit.
—His lack of connectedness with his past makes it difficult for him to
　　—carry a grudge (he forgives easily);
　　—remember a learned sequence or the instruction from yesterday;
　　—keep a promise honestly made;
　　—feel guilty *now* for behavior that is past.
—The nebulous future makes
　　—consideration of consequences most difficult;
　　—preparation now for a hazy tomorrow irrelevant;
　　—ideas harder to remember than things to *do*.
—Being here right now totally means
　　—you risk all of you all the time;
　　—failure is total and the reaction is total but the reaction doesn't last because
　　　　—pleasure is total also and there is little room for mixed feelings;
　　　　—you need to be first because now is your only chance;
　　　　—the need of the moment engulfs the total present and it is "all there is";
　　　　—promises made to occur after meeting conditions are vaguely joined with conditions and time.

He is unaware of the unspoken boundaries of personal space and personal time—and intrudes unannounced and is often unwelcome.

Racing with the Elbow

He stands at the line next to Fred, wrong foot forward. His face is twisted sideways to view Fred's right elbow. Fred won the last race and he figures it's the elbow pumping that gave Fred the extra speed. He bends his left arm to match Fred's right and is giving it a few practice swings. The arm moves stiffly, independent of his body.

His whole life is an attempt to match his performance to an external model—to an outside center—to expectations of others—and his life is a series of races ill-run, uncoordinated and alone. He never really finishes anything. It's over, won or unanswered, before the elbow is swinging right or even the first column added.

He smiles at his secret—the elbow will win—this time, yes, this time —and the signal to "get set" alerts the whole body—frozen—then remembers . . . the elbow! "Go!" He pumps it vigorously, runs a few steps, watching Fred's elbow, tries matching the rhythm, falls sideways and hard . . . left elbow still pumping as the right one bleeds.

He hollers, "Wait! Wait!" at Fred's elbow, but it disappears taking Fred with it.

A New View

One of the best ways to help is to assist parents and teachers toward a new point of view. Parents who view the child in terms of *his* world, instead of assuming his world is as theirs, develop a new kind of relating. Parents remain emotionally involved (as parents must be) but it leaves out condemnation of both the child and themselves. They can quit categorizing in terms of good and bad, right and wrong, all or nothing— see him in terms of the reactions stemming from a shared point of view. He develops from where he is to "where he's supposed to be." If you can genuinely appreciate him, then he can genuinely appreciate himself.

When parents and teachers give up the good and bad categories they take a more objective point of view. They develop a new way of relating and a new kind of interaction emerges.

> They stop walking on eggs.
> They don't have to be afraid of him anymore.
> They *allow* him to become more organized through structure, rather than imposing structure as punishment.

The Attitude Makes a Difference

If we can help the parent to get inside him to see that his motivation doesn't have to do with devils or badness *vs.* goodness but is a natural consequence of *his* view of the world, then we can focus on modifying the way he sees things. Right now, we don't look at his behavior and wonder how it seems to him; we see the behavior and evaluate in terms of how it seems to us—which is usually different.

Up to this point parents and teachers have been behaving toward him in terms of what their motivation would be if they behaved in the way he behaves. And they are unable to understand because they simply would not behave the way he behaves . . . with the kind of motivation with which they endow him. They are unable to fathom the basis

32

from which his behavior springs. It is this *basis* that we must *construct* because the child says very little about himself. He hasn't been able to tell us.

Parents and teachers are climbing the walls—and we see the child and we can't understand how this little kid generates such turmoil. The parents and teachers are sure he is doing it but they don't know *how*. We provide them with a new way of seeing him—by constructing his point of view from observations of him, the parents, and the teachers.

We asked them to spell out by situation and detail how they arrive at the conclusions they reach—that he is, for example, irresponsible, selfish, careless, and unpredictable. We have to give them a *why* that makes sense to them so they can assist this child to modify his behavior in terms of where he is now. These are some of the situations on which our conclusions are based.

Presenting: The Top Banana

The Situation: The child comes into the kitchen and says, "Give me a banana." The parent responds, "I think you've had your share. There were ten bananas and you've eaten eight of them and your little sister has not had any. Now—if you still want it—OK." So he eats it.

Mother's conclusion: He thinks only of himself. He is selfish.

Explanation: (The situation from the child's point of view) He does not see the connection between eating the banana as symbolizing unfairness or selfishness. He does not see his behavior of the past (having eaten eight bananas) as being connected with the need of the moment. That was then; this is now. And he has no concept of time. "I want a banana. She says I can have one. I get one."

Alternative: He says, "Give me a banana." The parent might say, "Take one," or the parent might say, "No, you've had your share." (The parent then sticks to the decision he makes and is not obligated to explain it to the child. After all, the parent is the main banana distributor.)

Presenting: What Time Is It?

The Situation: He loses his watch (also his coat, gloves, anything). He comes in asking, "What time is it?" (He is always asking about the time and asking you to tell him even though he is standing right next to the clock and he knows how to tell time. That's why you bought him the watch in the first place.)

Mother asks, "Where's your watch?"

"I don't know. What time is it?"

"Where did you leave it?"

"I lost it." (There is no sign that he feels bad about it.) He doesn't have it anymore, and that's it. He even says, "That's the second watch I lost in the past six months."

Mother's conclusion: He's careless.
He doesn't take care of his things.
Nothing means anything to him.
He doesn't even feel guilty.

Explanation: Possessions do not become a part of him. Possessions are to be used when you need them at that moment. Things that he doesn't need right now aren't important because he has no future. They are only important at the time. Things happen *to* him; he doesn't make things happen. He didn't do it; he is not responsible; he doesn't feel guilty.

Presenting: The Ingrate

The Situation: Mother comes down and fixes breakfast. She makes oatmeal because not too long ago the child said he sure would like to have oatmeal someday. So this is a labor of love, and he is to be surprised with a bowl of hot oatmeal sprinkled with brown sugar and butter. She is expecting some appreciation for her efforts and recognition that she went out of her way to please him. He comes downstairs. She says brightly, "Would you like a nice bowl of hot oatmeal with brown sugar and butter?" He answers matter-of-factly, "Nope." Mother replies. . . . (Well, what would *you* say?)

Mother's conclusion: He doesn't appreciate anything I do for him.

Explanation: He was given a choice—and he thought it was a real choice. He did not see the choice as being an opportunity to express gratitude, but simply as a choice of having or not having a bowl of oatmeal. He is not aware of mother's ulterior motivation—the seeking of a response indicating appreciation of her efforts. He doesn't even remember asking for oatmeal once.

Alternatives: Mother: "I fixed oatmeal. Here's yours." (He is very likely to accept it. If he doesn't, it is because he doesn't want oatmeal, not because he doesn't want you.)

Advice to parents: Do not confuse yourself with a bowl of oatmeal. If you want to know if he loves you, ask him directly and you'll get an honest answer, but know it is only for that moment.

Presenting: "Never mind: I'll do it myself"

The Situation: The trash basket is full. It's his job to empty it. He hasn't even noticed. You think to yourself he's a lousy kid, but you're willing to modify your hypothesis so you give him an opportunity to be a good kid. You give him the illusion of choice, hoping that *this* time at least he will demonstrate he is a social animal. And you say, "Would you like to carry out the trash?" "Nope," he says, matter-of-factly. You are not easily discouraged. Maybe he didn't get the message. So you say it more directly, "Would you like to carry out the trash for mommy?" Response, "Nope," (matter-of-factly.) Mother, through her teeth, "Even though I worked all day cleaning the house, making your bed, washing and ironing your clothes, fixing you hot oatmeal for breakfast, to the point where I'm ready to drop—in spite of all this—I'll carry out the trash." The child says, "OK," matter-of-factly.

Mother's conclusion: He's irresponsible because it was his job to carry out the trash in the first place.

Explanation: Explanations can come only after you've cooled off. He misses the message that mother is trying to give him. He doesn't see that carrying out the trash has anything to do with making mommy feel good. If you give him a choice—he believes he has a true choice—no strings attached. He doesn't respond to our emotional blackmail.

Alternative: Tell him, "The trash basket is full. Carry it out and burn it now." (He is very likely to say OK, matter-of-factly.) He reacts to the direct message.

Presenting: Whatdoyawantfromme? ! ? !

The Situation: He comes to you five minutes before it is time to leave for school. He says, "I've got to build a farm. I need all kinds of stuff." (You're relieved to hear it's just a play-like farm.)
   "What do you need to build a farm?"
   "Oh, I don't know—just the stuff."
   "Like what?"
   "Like some little animals and stuff to build a barn out of—and something for grass and I guess I'll build it in a big box."
   "When do you have to have it?" (You figure you have at least a week.)
   "We're going to do it this morning."
   "You gotta be kidding. Why didn't you think of this last night or the day before? Where am I going to find all this stuff? You think this is a department store?"
   "I need some scissors and paste, too."
   Strangely enough, his mother starts getting things together—enough to satisfy him. He says, "Bye mom . . . going to school now." She collapses, muttering to herself. "He did it again."

Explanation: He does sort of remember what he is supposed to do but not on time. Time has little meaning. He doesn't see the connection between gathering the materials and doing the task because he is not aware of the order of events that must take place for a task to be completed. He is certainly not aware that these events take place in a time-dimension. And he didn't need them last night. He only needs them now. And you came through. If you can, you do, and if you can't, you don't.

Presenting: One More Chance

The Situation: The family is having supper. *He* doesn't like what he has been served. He complains; he pokes his brother next to him. The mother says, "Eat it." He says, "I don't want it." The other kids laugh. Then he makes faces and wiggles. They laugh some more, and he still refuses to eat. Soon the parents lose their control, everyone is getting out of hand, and *he's* doing it. So they threaten that if he doesn't straighten up he will have to leave the table. He says he will, but he doesn't straighten up. He plays with his food, starts it again, even though he promised. Mother makes a move toward him and he says, "Give me one more chance, I'll stop." She does. He doesn't. This time she gets out of her chair and starts toward him. Everybody is laughing as she is chasing him. She sits down embarrassed and disgusted and says, "Stan, *you* take over." He gets him and spanks him and puts him in his room. *He* comes down later after supper is over acting like nothing happened.

Mother's conclusions: He's a comic, a clown, a troublemaker.
Makes me feel like a failure as a cook.
Makes me feel like a fool for having chased him.
Makes me feel bad because he got a whipping;
   my husband went too far. He wouldn't be
   the way he is if I were a better mother.
He doesn't have the decency to say he's sorry.
He doesn't feel guilty at all. He comes down-
   stairs to watch *his* TV program because it
   is *his* turn.
(She can be sure he'll do it again tomorrow.)

Explanation: What happens to him in a group? He seems to use the same techniques with the mother in a group as when he's alone with her. He doesn't have the concepts of sharing, taking turns, being considerate. He doesn't need them when he's alone with her with nobody to share. He is always the STAR—even in a company of players. He never plays a supporting role. He gets top-billing.

Alternatives: Send him to his room—so you can be comfortable. Do it when he starts because it is not going to stop, even if he promises to "be good." Feed him earlier or later when the situation is not complex. You can try him back with the family to see if he can make it. You can ask him if he wants to eat with the family tonight or by himself. He'll tell you depending upon how he is feeling.

Presenting: You Want Me to Be Successful, Dontcha?

The Situation: He is in junior high and he swipes musical instruments and teachers' answer books. He makes no attempts to hide it. His counselor says, "He sort of borrows things," but he suspects that he should call it stealing.

He talks to the boy. He explains that you don't do that, you don't take what belongs to other people. That's stealing. The child says, "I needed it—so I took it. What's wrong with that?" And he seems genuinely puzzled. The counselor doesn't know whether to believe him or not. "Is he putting me on?"

Explanation: As always, he responds to his need of the moment. People want him to do well—he wants to do well—and that means he has to have the right answers. He doesn't know them so he has to get them. He is sure the teacher would want him to have them. So he takes them —borrows them? What does that mean—stealing?? And the instrument? If somebody needed his, he would give it to him, of course.

A Child's View

How Does the Child View the World?

THE CHILD SPEAKS WITH STRAIGHT TONGUE

Believe him. He is puzzling because he *is* as we see him. There is a strong possibility that he is so *uncomplicated* we cannot easily understand it.

HE DOES NOT HAVE ULTERIOR MOTIVES

He is direct. There is no indirect to him. Something seems to be missing that prevents him from acquiring the skills which would permit him to play the ordinary social games that we play with each other.

What is lacking? The capacity for seeing the shadings. He misses the indirect, and so misses the subtleties, the implications. For example, he doesn't know that you depend on him for you to feel good. He doesn't know that eating the oatmeal you fixed is a way of making you feel good. He thought it was for him. But you assume that if he doesn't eat the oatmeal he knows it is a way to make you feel bad. He doesn't perceive what you need, unless that need is obvious, something he can see. It goes both ways with him.

> "You need something—here."
> "I need something—give it to me."

He doesn't often *ask* for things. Instead, he *tells* you what he wants, and he expects you to give it to him. He seldom says, "Thank you." He acts as if he deserves everything he wants; he has a natural right to it, and if he lets you know that he needs it, wants it, he will receive it. He expects to get it. It doesn't seem to him that anyone ever does him a favor.

HE SEEMS TO THINK ONLY OF HIMSELF

He doesn't seem to care—and that means you don't have any weapons for controlling him. You can't win with him, you can't con him. We are busy much of the time trying to "psych" him out, but the child is not encumbered by that labor.

HE IS A GREAT BEHAVIOR MODIFIER!

He doesn't feel powerful as you think he does. He doesn't feel that he has manipulated, because he didn't plan it that way. He really does not have ulterior motives.

He is powerful because he has no power. He lives mostly for the moment. He understands *now*—not yesterday or tomorrow. When he does something we don't like and we ask him what he thought would happen, he doesn't know because he doesn't consider the consequences —because he deals only with the present. He does not carry the past with him. He doesn't know about tomorrow until it gets here.

TIME IS NOT THE SAME FOR HIM AS IT IS FOR US

Events are not connected in time for him. He is not trapped by his past as we are—and his present is not molded by the consequences of the future. (How could he possibly fit our definition of "responsible behavior"?)

HE DANCES TO A DIFFERENT TUNE

He waits until the last minute to ask for something and is unaware of the time it will take to meet his demand. He doesn't know about the time and preparation that precedes an event. There's no sense of cause and effect. He doesn't know about sequence—the steps it takes to arrive someplace. Sequence is ordered events—doings strung out in time.

Possessions do not become a part of him. He is not distraught when he loses something—until he needs it again.

HE DOESN'T FEEL GUILTY

We feel that he has it too easy—he suffers only at the moment. He doesn't carry it with him all the time. He doesn't understand the basis on which you are expressing your anger. He fails to see that it stems from his behavior. What did he have to do with it? When he asks, "What are you mad about?" he isn't trying to shift the blame. He is asking an honest question. He doesn't know. Long explanations about his responsibility do not clarify the matter for him. We are as puzzling to him as he is to us.

HE'S SO IRRESPONSIBLE

He can't put himself in your place with your feelings. We burden him by giving him choices. We give him the opportunity of making the "right" choice, which is the one that will please us, but he doesn't see it from that point of view. He seems tactless, insensitive because he doesn't know that he is obligated to make us feel good.

HE DOESN'T PLAY SOCIAL GAMES

He has trouble getting started with a task. He has trouble finishing a task, and yet he has to have closure—some things he will keep at half the night. He loses organization with surprises.

HE'S SO UNPREDICTABLE

In the same way he forgets his spelling words or where he puts his book, he might walk away from something he is eating and forget about finishing it. He might not think about it again until he sees someone else eating. Then, he wants some, too, and he examines everyone's plate to see who got the most.

HE ALWAYS HAS TO BE FIRST

He doesn't hold a grudge. He forgives and forgets easily. There is not too much to talk to him about; everything is settled in a hurry. He appears to be naive and gullible and is easily led or misled.

In view of all that has been said, this child *does* have a structure that he follows:

HE LIVES ONLY FOR THE MOMENT

Finding a Way

If the job is to be done, parents and teachers must do it. And they must do it within the boundaries of the possible. To make recommendations requiring equipment, knowledge, or skills out of their reach is to increase their sense of helplessness and frustration.

To blame parents and teachers is to deny responsibility. To label the child is not to solve his problems. We should be *sharing* with parents and teachers, not telling them. They are not puppets to carry out recommendations imposed on them, but rather should choose actions based on their own understanding.

A Father Looks

He never turns the lights off in the basement, ever. He doesn't turn just one on—he turns them *all* on. You go down there the next day and they've been burning for hours. So I say to myself, "OK, every night before he goes to bed tell him to go down and turn the lights off." Then suppose I forget to tell him to turn the lights off—then it's my fault? He doesn't take any responsibility. If it would be just that, it wouldn't be so bad—but it's not just that—it's many, many things. Maybe if I choose just one—work on it—focus on that. If I see progress in that one thing maybe it will give me the courage to live another day. But if I try to tackle it all at once, it's hopeless. How do I get myself into such messes with him? He's got me in over my head all the time. I'm off-balance. I can take cold showers, I can go for a walk, I can smash a window, I can do myself a favor by giving up one of my hobbies so I'll have more time for him! ! !

He never finishes anything. You know part of the reason he never finishes anything? Because I let him start too many things. His needs are of the moment. He comes in—"Can I go to California—take pottery lessons—play the trumpet?" Last night he asked me to join the bowling league with him. He wants to get some pigeons—he wants a bow and arrow—he wants to make a clubhouse. He thinks he'll save his money for a tent. And he's got those horses that I board in the country that he never thinks of. Part of the reason he doesn't finish things is that he has too much going.

Why does he have too much going? Because he never sees anything that he doesn't want. He never hears about anyone doing something that he doesn't ask to do himself. He's at me all the time wanting something, so I'm having a hard time saying "no." A couple things happen. He hits upon something that I kind of think I might like, too. Like the pigeons. I thought that might be fun—before I found how much work there is to it. So some of the things I latch onto because I want to do them. So I get enthusiastic, and I buy materials and I build things—and I do all the work and I really invest in it and I do it for the kid all the time. After a while he's not interested—he's off somewhere doing something else, and there I am, sweating over those pigeons or horses or dogs or whatever, and he's off figuring another three-year project. Happy as a lark. And there I am stuck. He's not taking care of anything.

But the other thing is that I start feeling guilty because I say "no" so much. So one day he says, "How about a trip to Europe?" I tell him "no!" Well, then, he asks, "How about a trip to California?" I think that's reasonable compared to a trip to Europe; besides, I turned him down on a trip to Europe yesterday, so I'll say "yes"—I don't want him to think I don't love him. I don't say "yes" very often, but I have to remember that he asks for a million more things than most kids. So even though I haven't said "yes" very often, I've said "yes" more than anybody ever should. When I say "no," I notice that it doesn't make him feel very bad—but it makes *me* feel bad to say "no" so much.

Whatever he does, he leaves a bunch of strings hanging out wherever he's been; nothing is ever finished and clean.

So, what's the answer—what are the alternatives? First, I start by listening to myself and recognizing that that's the way it is—that I feel guilty, that I don't need to feel guilty; that I say "yes" too often, that he doesn't need me to say "yes" that often.

Once you realize it, what more do you have to do? Does it mean that then, automatically, you are going to behave differently?

What do you think would happen if I would choose one thing and check on it? He'd start doing it. But what happens is that there is so much that needs changing that it looks hopeless. I keep trying to do everything at once, but I can't—and so I really can't see that I'm making any progress. It makes sense to pick out one thing—something that has some possibilities so that he can be successful. You focus on that and help him focus on that until it becomes automatic. It has to be something that happens often enough so he gets into a habit.

Well, I help him remember. I know he has trouble remembering. It's not his fault and it's not my fault, but it is important for the lights to be turned off in the basement. It's an automatic habit that needs to be developed. And so I'll help him to remember for awhile. See if he learns it. If he does, I'll feel good and if he doesn't—and if he doesn't, I'll just keep telling him, and eventually he will. Sometime he will.

The Guilt Merry-Go-Round

I was very relieved to learn that maybe his difficulties stemmed from something other than my being a terrible mother. But because of the way he is, I do develop a good deal of irritation with him. And then I think that my irritation with him caused him to be the way he is, and I feel guilty and try to make up for it. He doesn't come through, he doesn't appreciate my being nice, and then I get angrier than ever and I think, "If I could just stop being angry at him then he wouldn't be so upset," and after a while I'm at some absurd extreme and really out of control.

What have I done to make him the way he is? I'm a terrible parent. I get broad hints from teachers and others that they think I am, too. They look sideways at me and ask, "How does he get along at home? Do you have any trouble with him there?" I know what they mean—all those suggestive questions that stir up guilt. So I try *harder* with this child—I give him more. I listen to him more. I treat him like he was more fragile so as not to upset him. I'm not as definite in what I say to him— I give him more choices. I ask him questions instead of telling him. And it gets even worse! With all my concern and trying to feel out what he wants that would make him happy, and I'm still failing—I finally get mad as hell at him. And I blow up at him. I ground him for years. I feel even guiltier—and then the whole thing starts over again.

The Task

*Isn't it normal
for children to
take on the values
of the family in
which they live?*

He sure doesn't see things from our point of view! And I'll be darned if I can figure out what *his* point of view is. It's as if we start everything from a different position and we end up being mad. He only thinks of right now. It's like he can't see it our way—not anything.

We've practically given up trying to get him to see it *our* way and if anything is going to be done it looks like we're going to have to see it *his* way. That's hard, because he doesn't have the same values we do. What he wants right now seems to be his only guide. He has no thought of whether or not he is justified. How he behaved yesterday or even a few minutes ago doesn't seem to matter. He has no regard for the consequences of his behavior. He doesn't seem to care what other people think; doesn't even seem to care about himself—whether or not he will have anything left for tomorrow. He acts like there was always more where it came from. Somehow, it's all so easy for him. He leaves pieces trailing behind him, and somehow, they get picked up by other people. He doesn't take any responsibility.

To know how he is is one thing—to accept it is something else. It's bad for us because it has to do with all our values, and our values are based on different dimensions of living. But we are mainly concerned with living with him and liking what he does. We're very worried about what is going to happen to him in the future—if he isn't able to learn to be a responsible human being. We can't change totally or entirely or all at once. It's going to have to be gradual, and we know that, too. If we could see just a little progress it would help. If we are going to teach him responsibility and teach him the consequences of his behavior then we've got to start way back where he is. We're thinking of things like helping him see some connection between feeding pigs in the summer and getting his check for selling them in the fall, and he is still back trying to predict what will happen if he kicks his older brother in the shins, and not doing too well with that. If we can start back where he is and then gradually expand it, maybe we can keep in step with him.

Part of what makes it difficult is his total reaction to frustration. When we correct him just a little bit, he reacts a whole lot. He reacts as if it were the end of the world, and I guess by the way he behaves that maybe it *is* for him. We see things in terms of the past and the present and the future while he invests everything in the moment. He wants something while I'm talking on the phone to a friend, and if I won't meet his need immediately he goes and beats on the tin table-top. I don't understand it, and I'm sure not able to ignore it. That's what I mean when I say he keeps me walking on eggs—I can never predict his reaction—it never seems to be in line with what you would expect. A lot of times I just give in to keep the peace and I guess maybe that's part of the reason he doesn't change because sometimes it works for him—and he, being an eternal optimist, thinks this is the time it is going to work. If he were a lot younger I could understand it better, because a lot of his behavior is comparable to a pre-school child. As he's gotten older we've expanded what we expect from him, but he's not expanded his ability to respond to what we expect. We get farther out of step.

It's really got us puzzled—we don't have any of these problems with the other children. We let them know what the rules of the household are, what our expectations are, what our values are, then they know that if you do this, that happens, and they develop responsibility. They handle it very well. They don't always like it, maybe, but they know what we expect. But it just doesn't happen with him. Doesn't he want to fit? Doesn't he want to be a member of our family?

I guess he simply doesn't see it our way. Maybe he isn't able to but that's awfully hard to remember. Most children seem to learn what is expected—automatically—just by living with you—because they want to please you. That's another thing about him, he doesn't seem to care whether he pleases us or not.

It's hard, really, to teach him. It's like we have to teach him things that we don't really know but we just expect automatically because it's part of being a human being. It's easier if I don't ask him to do something or give him a choice—it's easier just to tell him what to do and to tell him to do it right now. It works! If I change the way I say things to him, it does help him do differently. But, believe me, it makes me very uncomfortable—why should I have to behave like a Master Sergeant with my own child and give him orders—but it is the only way he will do it. He doesn't pick up anything by implication or innuendo or by subtlety—he can't deal with anything unless it is under his nose and I have him do it now.

There are so many questions. I know that he is different. But *how* different? Does he *feel* different from the rest of us?

At times there is not much happiness in our family. We feel pretty grim because we just can't make it go well with him. We can never forget that he is there. We are always aware of his presence and of our need to do something with him or for him or about him almost every minute of our lives. No matter what we plan for our family we usually have to plan it around him. And the others get angry because it really is not fair to everyone else. He gets more time, he gets more of my attention than anyone else, but it seems never to be enough and it doesn't seem to make that much of a difference. I feel like I'm cheating the other children. They respond, they say "Thank you," and they seem to

"It wouldn't be so bad if he were an only child."

appreciate what we do for them. Maybe we contribute to it because we are kind of afraid of him—we do kind of walk on eggs—with him—and let him be in the spotlight all the time—to keep peace.

I wish you could know how much time and money we have spent on him—just on school things. For example, we buy records on phonics, we work for hours on spelling. He gets it, but tomorrow it's like he never saw the word before. There is only so much time you have to give and he seems to need it all. He can't go off and play by himself, and I can't forget about him when he's draped around my neck all the time.

It's very confusing to us. The school says he has the ability to do better and so we figure that if he has the ability to do better then we are going to insist that he does better. We set aside a study time every night, we schedule him, we make lists so he doesn't forget and we see that he meets the responsibilities as the school sees them. We see that he responds at home, but when he gets to school the next day he gets the same reports sent back with him. They say that he didn't study, that he is not improving, that there isn't any sign of change or progress. It's frustrating.

It's frustrating for him, too. He says that we're on his back all the time. But the thing that really upsets us was the report that the school gave to the doctor—they told him that he would do better but that "the parents are on his back all the time." The doctor advised us not to put so much pressure on him! It would help a lot if everyone would get together and give us the same advice.

I know he gets tired doing homework, but when he gets started he's a hard worker. He has to whisper directions to himself all the time, and he gets a death-grip on that pencil. He's very tired when he gets through. He whispers instructions to himself trying to do everything right. When you see the work after he's finished—when he has all the time that he needs—it doesn't look too bad, but if you would watch the process, the procedure that he goes through to arrive at the finished product—you would see *labor*—you would see vast amounts of time consumed—it's not a smooth performance and you see a lot of uncertainty.

He doesn't remember his times-tables any better than he remembers to take out the trash. But if you ask him a question, he usually knows the answer. That must be why he does all right on intelligence tests—they say he has above average intelligence. But they just ask him a question and he gives an answer. There are no steps in-between to get him confused. You give him a task that requires him to start and to finish with a number of steps in-between, he doesn't know where to start and he doesn't know when he's through.

Everybody makes suggestions about what we can do but there are no guarantees that if we do them he will do better in school. We've given up hope that he's going to college. But what worries us most is how other people are going to learn to live with him. Is he ever going to develop any responsibility? Is he ever going to understand about consequences? Is he going to fit better in this family right now?

We've become convinced that he doesn't deliberately set out to bug us and knowing that makes a difference. It doesn't change everything, but it makes a difference. I guess we've come to expect the worst of him, and it's true, we've never told anyone how bad it is at home. I guess we don't tell because we feel that it must be our fault and we kind of cover up for him. I guess we are really covering up for ourselves. Since we figure it is probably our fault, we feel that maybe we deserve everything we get at home; but when he behaves badly in public and it's out in the open, we figure we can say, "OK, so it's my fault, tell me what to do to make it better. We don't like it this way either." Then what we get is contradictory advice.

Well, let me tell you, I'll bet you that anybody that lived with him would have difficulty!

We feel that we've collected as many red checkmarks as he has and about our only basis for relating to him is our failure together.

Maybe

If you can understand how it is with him—that–	Then you can–
he doesn't bug you deliberately	(sometimes) be less angry at him and at yourself.
he has no ulterior motives	give him direction more objectively and directly.
reactions are total but transitory	know that you need not match his emotional level.
saying "no" is not damaging to him	say "no" without being afraid.
he truly needs more time to learn values as well as times-tables	make your expectations match where he is.
he has trouble making choices and getting started	choose for him and point the way.
he loses organization under pressure	back off for the moment without feeling he has won.
he doesn't carry a grudge	forgive yourself if you blow up.
he has trouble with time and sequence	help him along the way, show him where to start.
he often doesn't know he needs help	give it without asking him or waiting for him to ask you.
he relates in terms of *now* because "yesterday" and "tomorrow" have less meaning for him than for you	be less bothered if he doesn't feel guilty.
he can't see it from your point of view	make an effort to see it from his point of view.

he is direct and honest in his approach	be direct and honest in your approach to him.
that he is telling you true and his questions are honest	answer without sarcasm.
he believes, when given a choice, that it is a true choice	give him honest choices.
he doesn't know you need something unless it shows	know that emotional blackmail won't work.
he doesn't know why you are angry—he doesn't connect it with his past behavior	not hold him responsible for your angry feelings.
he can't respond to your unspoken requests	say what you mean directly.
he truly doesn't know how to look for something	show him with tolerance.
he lacks a sense of ownership or possession—this depends on knowing the needs of tomorrow	tolerate his losses a *little* more gracefully.
he hurries through tasks before he forgets what he was supposed to do	re-define "carelessness."
he is puzzling because he *is* what you see	react to what is.
he truly wants to be successful	help him objectively.
he doesn't feel powerful	quit being afraid.
he functions better the less complicated the situation	provide simplicity when possible.
he doesn't change because he doesn't know how, unless you show him	show him.

*The task is to provide a
climate which allows you
to keep your sanity and
him to keep his
self-respect.*

When you know that his behavior stems from an inability to match your expectations and not in reaction to your "bad parenting," you no longer need engage in the fruitless contest of "forcing him to behave," being chronically and mutually disappointed.

You can use your energy to view with *his* view, to alter your expectations to those possible for him to meet. As he meets expectations, his respect for self and the feeling that he "fits" is matched by your confidence in setting new goals, and mutual blame becomes mutual joy. He comes "unstuck," more willing to explore and change and risk as the tragedies of yesterday are the "boo-boos" to learn by today.

He is freed from functioning as a positive or negative extension of others and develops internal directives based on self-valuation.

"He could if he wanted to" becomes "He wants to and can!"

Exploring with Parents

It's not easy to be a parent in this day and age, especially a mother; but more recently fathers also are receiving a larger share of the blame should the child function in such a manner as to make waves for one of the stalwart representatives of what-should-be.

Parents serve as a built-in excuse when any of the other social systems "fail" in their dealings with a child—they've done their best, "it must be his homelife." Parents really can't win. If the child is successful in meeting expectations outside the family, the outside expectors take the credit. It's only when he fails that the reliable stand-by gets called in for blame. This absurd situation develops until in early adolescence the child himself believes that everything "good" about him he did by himself and that everything "bad" is the parents' fault.

This view is so prevalent that most parents accept it as a "given." They come asking you to help them ferret out the ways in which they are damaging the child and confessing in detail every possible trauma or crisis of the past which might account for the child's difficulties. Unfortunately, those of us playing detective find much to latch onto that fits our preconceptions, and this makes it unnecessary for us to change our thinking. We just respond to the notions that fit and soon the parents are picking up the cues as to what *we* think and are very busy providing elaborations in those areas we indicate by our smiles and nods. It's no wonder that parents become tangled, frustrated and defensive. They get a different story from everyone.

They take the child to be evaluated, and recommendations based on a few hours of observations are made in terms of the child's needs, not taking account of the emotional needs of the parents, the environmental situation in which they must function, or the needs of other siblings in the family.

They go away armed with a new set of recommendations that continue to place this child in the center of the family attention as if all others in the family existed only to serve him. Family resentment ("Why is *he* so important? !") grows and then they fear their resentment is going to make him worse.

Some recommendations given by professionals just don't work, especially those given in abstract terms. One of the most glaring examples was a report that said, "He must be given tasks that will make him less hyperactive—and training that will make him more responsible, and give him lots of praise." And parents come to use categories of "good and bad," and these labels also mask the specifics with which they must deal in daily living. If recommendations are given in generalities, parents fail to see the child as somebody who behaves in certain ways in certain situations at certain times.

Unlabeling occurs as we explore specifics with parents and they become able to make use of the vast store of information *they* have about the child. You learn very soon how important it is for you to *listen*.

Let them tell you. Listen with an open mind and delay categorizing information into causes and effects. Most often the anxiety, concern, and frustration exhibited by parents are as much results as causes. For sure, they don't want it the way it is and if it can be different they are eager to learn how. The past is riddled with disappointment and most are engaged in the futile game of placing blame.

You can relate more effectively if you have spent some time with their child so you understand when they say, "At times, you couldn't ask for a nicer boy," for that has been your impression: cooperative, pleasant, willing to participate, eager to do his best in a one-to-one situation. You also know that many things are difficult for him. You've seen what he does and how he does it, and you've seen his reaction to difficulty. He makes excuses or quits or avoids or becomes highly verbal. He talks—on and on—partly to get away from the task and partly to help himself know what to do next, to give himself direction.

They, also, have experienced him positively when they have him alone. They are willing to consider the possibility that he functions better in uncomplicated situations instead of concluding, "He needs my undivided attention," or "He is selfish," or "He has an emotional problem."

They try to tell you very early that they gave and give to him because he can't seem to function without the giving. He can't get going unless they are with him to tell him what to do, and to show him the way. Their other children could function independently, but not him. They did for him because they felt, they saw, they knew somehow that it had to be. They are uncomfortable with it—they are ambivalent about it because he remains dependent and all their efforts seem never enough.

We imply that their giving is designed to satisfy their dark need to keep him dependent—that he is them, projected. "What is it within you that can't release this child?" Your direct experience with him corrects this impression and you know, as do they, there is something lacking in him—a void to be filled—he is different.

This child, given similar circumstances but different parents, would, in all probability, still have difficulties. Parents need to know that we have no evidence to support speculation that they "cause" him to be the way he is to satisfy an unconscious need to punish either him or themselves. Such theories are irresponsible and are an old play on the "someone to blame" theme. The very fact that professionals have developed over thirty-nine diagnostic labels suggests a very complicated, and almost certainly, multiply determined phenomenon. It seems patently absurd to assign or even to infer "blame," to generate guilt, in those very persons whom we are professing to assist. This sort of labeling and name-calling is every bit as destructive as are the labels directly pasted on the child with the glue of our middle-class values.

Parents need assistance from the very beginning—some more than others—to free themselves from their own nagging doubts concerning their competence and good will, to permit them confidently to explore with the child and try new ways of relating.

You listen and make it clear that the needs of the parents are of valid concern. Parents have the right to become angry, the right to relief, the right to care comfortably. They can relate more securely when their own self-esteem is not on the block.

Recognition that they care, without assigning blame, permits reports of differences as early as the first session. "I begin to see him differently. I don't get so angry with him and so I don't hate myself for being a bad mother. I can predict my boiling point before the explosion and can take steps to avoid a large part of the blast." They are managing him, often applying techniques they used before, only sooner and more objectively —"I'll send him to his room to calm him rather than punish him." "He needs to be away from us for awhile, and we sure need some relief from him."—It makes a difference, to him and to them.

Parents are pleasantly surprised, when telling him without the anger, being matter-of-fact, without all the verbiage that gives him a choice, that this new way results in conforming response. They say how it is, and it is. It really makes a difference when they become direct and quit walking on eggs.

Exploring with parents means finding out what is important and possible for them, in terms of their situation; in terms of matching their resources with the needs of their child. This means listening without making recommendations in terms of the "ideal"—like suggesting they buy him a trampoline because he needs motor development or recommending a private tutor if it's not financially possible. Recommendations have to be realistic and not a drain on the entire family. Knowing the needs encourages creative use of materials and resources at hand.

He doesn't become a different child in any total sense, but there are changes which are satisfying to the parent. It has to do with the way they feel about themselves, in living with and managing the situation, in being less angry with him and less critical of themselves.

Once parents see how it is from his point of view they come up with suggestions and possibilities without your saying a word. When parents arrive at actions based on their own understanding, they experience real pleasure—something more than mechanically following advice.

They come to see the child's point of view through their own descriptions: "I took him to the supermarket because he wanted to have a special valentine for his teacher, whom he likes very much. At the check-out counter a motherly lady had a package of candy bars and she offered one to John who barked, 'NO!' I was embarrassed; he was so rude and the lady was trying to be nice to him. I sent him to the car to wait—I was angry. Later, I lectured and demanded an explanation from him and he told me quite calmly, "We learned in school *never* to take candy from a stranger—it might be poisoned." And you underline *her* report that he "can't shift," which leads her to another example. She understands without condemning—can focus on *his* view and less on her own embarrassment. A "mistake" was made, used for new learning. She goes on to describe, this time with humor, another instance which focuses on his difficulty in discriminating between the real and the pretend: "We were having a wrestling match on the floor—the kids, my husband and I. I don't do that very often, but I felt sort of playful. My husband had me down on the floor and he pretended he wouldn't let me up. John watched the whole thing, but he stood on the edge of the group—didn't enter the game. I looked to him and said, 'Help me, help me.' Instead of pouncing on us, he turned, ran out the door to the neighbors and announced that his father was beating his mother. I was really surprised that he didn't understand. He had been on the scene from the start and everyone had been laughing. He reacted to my call for help—he missed the subtleties—he didn't know it was a game."

With understanding, real liking develops and the parents return the next week and say, "Things are better. I'm seeing him differently and it's easier."

They tell you, you underscore, and connections develop almost immediately—he becomes more predictable. They become more energetically involved as they experience themselves as contributing to his success and not blamed for his failure.

They soon forget they ever felt guilty for making reasonable demands —but there is a period of uneasiness when they doubt change is for sure—and they do experience set-backs but they are more able to cope. Difficulty is more realistically seen as arising out of complex situations or changes in routine rather than arising from the dark—inner—ulterior core of his or their unconscious. Situations can be simplified and routine re-established much easier than modifying inner factors that exist only hypothetically.

The parents learn to listen to the child when he says, "I don't want to go to church today," and know he's doubting his ability to sit still. They are able to understand, "I don't want to go to school today" in the same way as an inner state of uneasiness that can't be more precisely communicated. They listen and realize the child wants to be viewed in a positive way, that his motivation may not be to get out of a duty, but to avoid making himself look bad. So they send him or keep him home— either way, without anger.

While there is so much we don't know, we do know some things: these children have difficulty with time and space and changing their behavior to fit a new or more complex situation. They don't catch subtleties or nuances. They live mostly in the present having few connections with the past and they can't consider consequences in the future. They must be taught directly much of what other children learn automatically.

When parents expect what is possible, what is possible occurs. They sense valid change from defensiveness to exploring with him and they learn, as you've learned, that each offers much when all are on the same side.

He teaches you some advantages of discarding the arsenal of hurts from the past; that labels of yesterday can be writ fresh today; that mutual respect permits trying new paths with curiosity and joy, for less desperate stakes.

> *Take care of "right now"—that's*
> *all there ever is.*

Listen to parents and use their examples to

    —demonstrate differences between *their* concept of time and the child's concept of time.

    —show differences between their indirect view and the child's direct view.

—demonstrate absence of ulterior motives on the part of the child.

—connect time percepts with the generalized labels of "irresponsible," "careless," "selfish," "always has to be first," etc.

—replace general labels with specific-to-situation labels to allow the
child freedom to develop a trial and error approach.

—assist parent in becoming more tolerant of self—to quit walking
on eggs—to get off the guilt merry-go-round.

—help focus on structuring in terms of what's possible now; to
expand expectations as child develops.

—replace perceptions based on projection with explanations based
on attention difficulties; (for example: "He does it if I have
him by himself, so he has to have all the attention," is
perhaps an invalid conclusion. An alternative conclusion is,
"He does better the less complex the situation.").

—point up positive aspects of the child's functioning; for example,
he doesn't carry a grudge, isn't burdened by "the arsenal of
hurts from the past."

—demonstrate the direct approach, without anger, without dire
predictions, with limited choices.

Exploring with Teachers

Suppose you discover that the motivation you've attributed to the child turns out to be that way *because* of your labeling and not because he was really that way?

Suppose "going fast before I lose it" is defined by you as "careless." "Going fast before I lose it," *becomes* his definition of "careless." It is shorter, more convenient, and in agreement with you. And so instead of a "going fast before I lose it" person, he becomes a "careless" person.

That gets different feedback from others. From a person who cares he becomes a person who doesn't care. People who "go fast before I lose it" care—the other kind care less.

"I go slow so I can get it right" changes to "he doesn't *want* to finish his work." "I try to pay attention to everything," changes to "he doesn't pay attention to anything," for what is viewed as inattention may very well be unfocused attention to all. Then you become right and he becomes predictable in terms of your labels as he comes to accept them. But he certainly doesn't like them—he's defensive and denies the labeling even before you accuse.

Is it possible that every child truly wants to be successful? You get that impression from kindergartners, from first-graders, most second-graders, and a lot of third-graders. By fourth grade, it finally begins to soak in: "Ah Ha! The reason I don't do well in school is because I don't want to! What took me so long to learn that! ! ! The reason I can't read is because I'm labeled a poor reader. Now, what was so tough learning that?" "I can't spell, I can't do math, and I don't care." "For all the years left, I go to school, not doing assignments requiring skills I don't have because I don't care."

Children get stuck on our labels, labels become libels, heavy as lead. They don't like it, so change it. Let them move toward success.

It is easier to communicate the child's world to the parent than to anyone else. Parents know how it is, but most haven't been able to formulate or organize their puzzling observations. The child's actions have been upsetting and unpredictable because no connecting links were available to make sense of behavior from situation to situation.

> "He's OK if I have him alone, but he is terrible in a group—just can't sit still—talks all the time—can't take turns."
> *is interpreted as*
> "He has to have all the attention—he won't share—he's selfish—only thinks of himself."

This characteristic is noted also by the teacher who, with the parent, has tried reasoning and encouraging the child to "be good." He is OK when alone with the teacher and the school psychologist has found him cooperative and attentive in the individual testing session. This very commonly noted characteristic often results in:

> "He's OK with me—what's wrong with the teacher?" "He must not get enough attention at home; he must be emotionally disturbed, he's so spoiled and demanding in a group." "He's never been taught to share."

And everyone gets on different sides.

Basically, the task remains for everyone, parents, teachers, and children, to get on the same side, try some things, and see if they work. It helps the teacher to have some understanding of this child and how he views the world. You have to be willing to listen to the different story that every teacher has to tell and to see it empathically from all points of view. Changes occur, sometimes rapidly, with no more than a change of attitude. That's the key to the whole thing: not only attitude toward the child, but as important, attitudes of teachers toward themselves.

The school psychologist looks for information to foster understanding. You don't collect information to use as ammunition to condemn. The teacher presents you with a whole mass of material, it pours out and you recognize that she feels overwhelmed. There is much that needs to be done and she's been thoroughly frustrated in trying to cope. At first, the teacher cannot listen. She is flooded with her feelings of failure with this child. The child needs structure and realistic expectations, but how is she going to provide them? If there is a personality conflict, perhaps it has come about because the child has given her so much trouble, and she hasn't known what to do about it. You have to provide for structure, but you have to allow flexibility for his differentness. You have to convey that he *can't*, not that he *won't*. You try some things and see if they work. Let the teachers know that their comfort is also of concern. Don't try to change everything at once. If you make suggestions, you pick out one thing for them to focus on and you select something you think might be possible.

It is appropriate to deal with the present, and "unlabeling" is a primary task if change and development are to occur. The label stops the trial and error play that characterizes informal learning. The negative labels that one collects in life account for, and are in direct proportion to, the sense of effort with which one performs life's duties—the sense of "trying" to perform, "in spite of," inadequacies.

Teachers, like parents, experience the child as a puzzle. He's unpredictable, and his behavior seems sprung from a source all his own. Their wants, needs and actions seem not meshed with his and they travel on parallel rails—often going in opposite directions, or if in the same direction at very different speeds. His performance and their expectations are viewed as miles apart and each is a mystery to each. But most puzzling of all—sometimes he comes through beautifully.

An approach that allows exploration is to ask for examples of behavior and then to examine with the teacher those situations and circumstances which make it most possible for him to perform adequately.

In summary, it is helpful to teachers if you

—look in the present for answers and not in the past for causes
—tell the story from all points of view so each can see how it is with the other
—give direction in terms of specific examples and not in generalities
—whenever possible, use the material they give you in presenting the specifics. (Usually they give you so much material that you don't have to look elsewhere!)

The behavior in individual versus group situations reflects the child's difficulty in focusing attention in complex or unstructured situations. It has to do with difficulty in ordering the steps necessary to complete a task and deciding "what should come first."

One boy, when given an arithmetic study assignment in class, would open his desk-top and stare. The teacher assumed he was daydreaming and then discovered, when she asked, that he was trying to decide what to do first. The parents were puzzled also, because he could do the problems at home in his room—if the mother sat him down and got him started.

The difficulty in sequencing events along a time continuum results in descriptions such as, "He never finishes his work," which means difficulty in getting started, or having consciously to direct every movement or motion because motor patterns are not automatic.

Many of these children need to "whisper instructions to their hands" as they perform writing or drawing tasks because many cannot derive "meaning" from a visual stimulus and must laboriously translate it into auditory segments. In the same way, some must vocalize to themselves as they read to derive "sense" from the visual squiggles. These children suffer especially after third grade when reading "aloud" is discontinued. They "whisper" as they read, and get disapproval from peers and teachers because they "mutter to themselves."

They are either highly verbal or very terse children. Some pour out a barrage of words that becomes more pitched as they use this mode to share experiences with you. They can tell you about an exciting event of the immediate past with elaborate and detailed repetition of the exact words exchanged, stopping to correct themselves if they discover omission of any detail, reliving the feelings that accompanied the original experience. They don't notice your subtle hints of boredom. They look directly at you, and may suddenly stop in the middle with, "I'm tired of telling this."

Difficulty in relating in a group situation stems also from carrying over the same ways of relating individually to relating in the group. The child stays focused on the teacher and answers all the questions "as if he were the only one." This inability to shift is viewed as, "He always has to be first," "He never gives anyone else a chance," "He won't take turns," "He disrupts the whole class."

Teachers have discovered that designating the student who is to reply to a question before asking the question, eliminates much disruption. If the teacher begins with, "Who knows—?," and *he* knows, he *says* immediately.

The intensity with which this child reacts, both positively and negatively, stems partly from the fact that he does not connect events in time. Knowledge that he answered that last question (in the past) and so should give someone else a turn now, has little meaning because *then* is not meaningfully connected to *now*. The fact that he will get a turn later is an event in a future that is yours but not his. He is more totally invested in *right now* than most children. He "wins" or "loses" more totally and reacts more intensely. This results in descriptions such as, "He can't stand to lose," "He's a very poor sport," "When he wins, he really rubs it in."

Another observation is, "He never finishes—he works so slowly." This contrasts with, "He rushes through his work." He is described as "careless, messy," because "he does everything so *fast*! !"

If, before the child has accepted the "careless" label, you ask him why he goes fast, he says, "I have to go fast before I lose it." He has learned from experience that his knowledge is largely of the moment, that it must be acted upon *now* or it disappears into the disconnected past. This tendency is noted in children who spell every word perfectly today and have forgotten most by tomorrow. As one child expressed it, "I get 'em, and then they fly away like butterflies." Later he concluded, "Other kids don't do that. I must have a poor memory."

These children actually try harder than others because it takes work just to stay focused on a task. They become indignant when, as it frequently happens, the teacher says, "You didn't study." It seems very reasonable to the teacher that a child missing ten out of twenty words, especially if this is an "easy" list, couldn't have studied much. The teacher becomes indignant when the child insists, "I got 'em *all* right before I left home this morning." This is often quite true.

The teacher is overwhelmed by the professionals' recommendations for remediation. If she follows all the suggestions for this child, just when shall she teach the other thirty?

It is most valuable if the teacher understands how it is from *his* point of view. This is hard for the teacher because it is a difficult task to imagine a world composed only of the present.

Specific characteristics of these children are different each from each. They are described variously in the following ways:

—Hyper- or hypoactive
—Never finishing work, or finishing too fast
—Starting many projects but never finishing, or staying doggedly on one thing until you nearly lose your mind
—Math is their best or their worst subject but is seldom in any position except one of these extremes
—Handwriting is usually described as terrible as is spelling although oral vocabulary is frequently very good

So on and on in all possible combinations.

In spite of all possible exceptions and combinations of characteristics, personality descriptions given by parents and teachers are remarkably similar. In abstracting a concept to account for these shared observations, the difficulty with *time* is a basic ingredient shared by these children.

If you lack the ability to connect events in terms of past-present-future, past and future have no impact on present. Your behavior is then similar to the behavior of these children.

Imagine how it might change the way you label him if

This Observation	*is based on*	*This Understanding*
He never gives anyone else a turn.		Taking turns means spacing responses in time, having a sense of "I *had* my turn," or, "I'll get my turn later."
He promises to do his assignment, then looks out the window, walks around, doesn't do anything.		A promise involves knowing about future. (He acts like he has all the time in the world because he has no concept of how much time it will take.)
He won't do it unless I stand right over him.		He can't start, (begin at a definite point in time) or decide which to do first, (order events in a time dimension).
If I ask someone to erase the board, he's the first one up and does a beautiful job but makes the other kids jealous.		If he can see the beginning and end all at once (in the present), he doesn't get lost or sidetracked (in time).
He does everything so *fast,* he's careless!		Once he sees (in the present) he has to go fast, or "he loses it," in time.
He is so forgetful—he never remembers.		To "remember" you must connect an event of the past with a *time* in the future. He can't.
He's so active.		He tries to crowd all the doing into present—the present is all that exists for him.
He's jerky in everything he does.		His timing is off.
He never admits he's done anything wrong!		Events of the "past" are gone like the spelling words. "What's my behavior of 'yesterday' got to do with 'right now'?" (He's genuinely puzzled at your anger.)

He has no sense of responsibility.	To behave "responsibly" you must connect a promise of yesterday with an act in the future.
He loses everything.	To put something where you'll know where it is requires knowledge of need in the future. "Possessions" are not part of him unless he needs them right now.

The teacher's basic task is to provide an environment which permits children to focus and to learn. Recommendations having value for *all* children are most useful to the teacher. This eliminates the need to apply procedures separately and add to her frustrations.

The lowered self-esteem which accompanies repeated failure and the consequent labeling which prevents exploratory learning must be modified if children are to approach a functional level corresponding to their potential.

"These children" are harder to "crush" than most children, however. This is so because they do not respond to subtleties or sarcasm, are often not aware of the connection between the teacher's anger in the present and their behavior in the past. "What are you so mad about?" is a genuine question. They really don't know. They respond totally to your anger—feel crushed for the moment—but are soon over it though you may be still boiling. They "forget" to stay crushed and view each moment as new. This doesn't last forever, however, and when they finally get the message, it is learned only too well, for they can't shift attitudes easily.

They get stuck hard with, "I can't do what she wants—I'm no good as a student and maybe as a person," and their honest complaint of, "I can't," becomes an obstinate, "I won't!"

It is helpful to focus on the positive aspects of achievement instead of the negative aspects of failure. A simple technique like emphasizing *adequacy* with a red checkmark, grading papers in terms of number *correct* instead of number wrong would be helpful. Most children report about a spelling test, "I got four wrong," and they feel disheartened. Reporting, "I got sixteen right," it much more encouraging.

This positive emphasis is helpful to all children but especially to *these* children. They have more difficulty than most seeing performance in the present as better than performance in the past. It is also more difficult for them to grasp the subtleties of *partial* success or *partial* failure—so "failing four items of twenty" is "failing" for them. They are more totally encouraged by partial success and more totally discouraged by partial failure.

If their performance on a task today could be compared with their performance on a similar task in the past, and their progress emphasized, their response would be much more positively goal directed. "Positive feedback" reinforces the main driving force toward a goal (spelling correctly) because there is joy at performing in accord with a goal. Feeding back "number wrong" changes the goal and it becomes learning to spell to escape threat of failure. Negative feedback increases anxiety, further disrupting the learning process, and learning becomes directed toward "pleasing the teacher so she won't clobber me," rather than "doing better today because I'm learning to spell to please me."

For these children, connecting performance *today* with performance in the *past* is vital. They can't automatically make connections through time.

Quit sending home failing papers for parents to sign—to witness *his* failure, to excuse your failure to teach. If a child misses thirteen of fifteen items on an assignment, there is something wrong with the assignment—not the child.

Send home a paper from the past with a better paper from the present —have the parent sign and witness "degree of success." You have happier parents, more eager kids and *your* success as a teacher is made gloriously obvious!

I Love You Leland

Observations are made in terms of a theory, in terms of our cultural norms. We are ever handicapped by our confusing "what is" with "what ought to be." We develop a theory and then the theory directs our perceptions. We can never be sure if our dream fits the theory or whether the theory generated the dream.

There is conflict in offering service to others when you've gone to school and learned how to serve. Sometimes people don't seem to need what you have. Do you teach them to need what you've been taught they *should* need? Or can you look more directly and change what you do to fit what you and they see? Do you confine your service to "those who can benefit" and wind up seeing yourself over and over? Or do you learn from these kids to "look now at this moment" in time.

These puzzling children are not puzzling if you have a theory and force them to fit. "It's hereditary." "It's psychogenic." "It's their perceptual training." "It's a combination." "The parents' fault." "The teacher's fault." "He just doesn't care." These hypotheses serve little purpose unless someone figures a way to reverse the birth process.

We are ready to go somewhere else. There is more excitement ahead. What becomes of these kids? They seem to disappear after they've gained self-esteem and they forget there was ever anything wrong in the first place.

You see that with parents when things go better. I remember calling Mrs. B. about David. She seemed surprised that I'd asked. She had forgotten how it had been with him. Parents forget not only about the past with him, but also about their own worry and guilt.

There is something sad about fitting in too well. You find that few pay attention. It's like quitting drinking if you've been a drunk. You get rewarded for awhile for *not* doing something. Life gets a trifle dull when people quit rewarding you when you don't do. That can't last too long, rewarding what *doesn't* happen. So maybe some people raise hell just to re-establish excitement and get a little reward when they quit again. Maybe that's what happens if you live for others and become dependent on them to say you're right or you're wrong. It's better to have the reward system inside of you.

Maybe that's why so many of these kids grow up to be very successful or totally unsuccessful. They have spent a long time performing for others, out of touch with the insides of themselves, *trying, driven,* to match their performance with the ideas of others. Their focus shifts in an all-or-nothing manner, from focus on self to focus on expectations of others.

The sameness they seek for acceptance must do something to them, eventually. Routine, dull sameness is developed to be "like the others." Once they reacted freshly for all was ever new, just the present. They reacted immediately to the shiny, the different, the detail, and often embarrassed others by their honest response.

It's almost certain that one of these kids fingered the king whose clothes were made visible only to those who were "good." They shouted right out, "Hey! That guy ain't got no clothes on! !" They aren't phony. They see it, they say it, and tact isn't in them.

"Looka this ma, and this ma, kin I have it? I want that one—see it? No, take it away"—and that's "hyperactive" because you're always miles behind as you figure "yes-no," "right-wrong" to a request or behavior of moments ago. They are busy making requests *now*, have forgotten they asked. You've said "no" so often you finally say "yes." They don't even remember that they asked. They don't feel guilty, but you do. It seems to go on forever and you're tearing your hair out.

They change, and you miss them the way that they were. It's funny to miss being told "I hate you" directly. Others think it but express it more indirectly. For them it is said, done, and over in a brief space of time. You are still fuming and boiling and they've forgotten they've said it. It was just for the moment. They leave the past behind, and let you leave it, too.

All the time, all the trouble, all the heartache and searching. The investment of self, though negative, adds to their importance. It's like putting all your money in a bank that always teeters on the brink of going broke and wiping you out. You may not like it, but you damn sure are interested and excited about the outcome. Forever they carry big hunks of you in them. Big hunks of worry and big hunks of your heart.

You're proud to say, "The whole band was out of step but him!" You know the tune that he marches to, the tune of right now.

He forgets polite niceties, the subtle build-up, but if you *really* need he sees that you do. He gives all he has, (you think generosity—you've been fooled again). His tomorrows have no more impact than does his conception of tomorrow for you.

When things don't work out, they don't work out. It's not even that he thought that they would. Things are a mess now—("Whatdaya mean, I caused it??"). He hollers and shouts when he's mad right now. He asks and he asks directly, assuming he'll get it. His askings and gettings in the past just don't count. "What's that got to do with now, Dum Dum?" His "Come here!" is responded to automatically, for he asks in a tone that leaves you no choice. As you rush to respond you wonder why you are doing it. You have a choice but he acts like you don't! You feel more like his servant, his cook, or his maid. You stop to remind yourself, "I'm his *mother*, he's s'posed to mind me! !"

Even if he knows only a little, people think it's a lot. He presents with such certainty there is no room for doubt. He thinks others are OK. He doesn't scheme and connive and doesn't see it in others. Sometimes when you don't expect bad, sure enough, it's not there.

How come he likes animals and brings them all home? Picks up and examines even *dead* toads, then wants to dry dishes without washing his hands? "I don't wanta do it—I got me a plan, let me keep it. OK. Gimme a kiss, mom!"

And when he's independent and making it on his own, what will you do with the hours of time left? You've given up hobbies and clubs and devoted so much to psyching him out. It's kind of a let-down to discover that it's his utter simplicity that was the whole puzzle.

The Last Page

Achieving a percept is a process of organizing stimuli—the *moment* of organization is made durable if it is accompanied by an "Ah ha!" This suggests that an affective experience is necessary to "fix" a percept. "Ah ha!" is *joy* in achieving structure—"I did it"—compared to the being directed by, which robs the self of doing, thus of joy, and performance becomes mechanical with joy or anger or sadness residing outside the self in another. To rob others of their *Ah ha*'s is to rob them of their humanity and they become faceless automatons marching in their routines toward death.

One cannot shift or choose to dance out of step so that, at best, they become "obsessive-compulsives" who even play ritualistically; at worst, they become "autistic"—a totally invested-in-others person because self does not exist.

"Work" is functioning as an extension of the wishes of others—of investing performance—evaluation functions—"meaningless" because the "meaning" is not-a-part-of-self.

"Play" is functioning in the service of the self and owning your "Ah ha's!"

Work can be a functioning with others toward goals whose desirability is agreed upon. Most work has overt and covert goals which means "performing but producing minimally"—making bubbles with very loud clanging noises—or building anvils in silence. Process-appropriate-to-goal depends not only on what you are making but also for whom you're making it—yourself, another, or both-of-us.

part 2

Reason for Distress

I am referring George because he needs help for his disturbed mental state and our classroom needs help because he disturbs us. George is

"When I have him alone . . .

but in a group!"

going nowhere academically this year. He gets along well with no one. George seems quite emotionally disturbed. He lies, swears, fights, yells, pouts, slams things, has tantrums, destroys school property, is wild, wild-eyed, smart-mouthed, aggressive, belligerent, negative, almost violent, potentially violent, sniveling, complaining, rebellious,—and not too difficult to reach in a special attention situation.

Same Song—Second Verse

The authors' rationale is uncomplicated and allows the conceptual integration of a child's functioning in both family and school. It leads directly to understanding and modification and requires neither etiological postulates nor assignment of blame. And in this complicated world, an uncomplicated rationale should find a welcome—especially from the theoretically uncommitted.

Stated simply, disorganization stems from a failure in sensory integration resulting in a present orientation, an inability to play social games, and a disconcerting directness that shatters social masks. Those affected tend to be loners, or to be the whole show. They do not keep track of favors or of disservices. They are one-to-one even in a group. They tend to react to your sacrifices matter-of-factly. They tend to report verbally in detail, find it hard to summarize or relate just to the main theme. They report without inserting judgment and usually without prejudice.

This failure in sensory integration varies in degree depending on the nature and complexity of the system with which the individual's performance must mesh and is as much determined by the situational requirements as by the state of the organism. Modification of expectations leads to integration as "performance demands" match "response potential."

Most integrational difficulties stem from sequential and con-sequential difficulties in the motor, visual, or auditory channels; or in the variation in self-concept arising from the early hyper or hypo reaction to touch.

Personality functioning can be described in sensory-perceptual terms and in terms of the internalization of labels applied by significant others when describing performance.

Conclusions based on direct observations are more directly beneficial in terms of modifying functioning than are conclusions which filter observations through preconceived theories or notions.

Functioning is more accurately described as an interactional result of all system elements than as resulting from a single element designated most potent. Thus, the terms *learning disability* or *teaching disability*, which assign potency to single aspects of an interactional system of needs and expectations, by virtue of the labeling act, assign blame.

School and academic problems are not separate from home and emotional problems. Often the school is unaware that parents are as concerned as they are. Parents are reticent in sharing family difficulties with schools because "trouble in the home" is the traditional explanation when school functioning is viewed as inadequate. (If the child's I.Q. goes up, the school did it. If it goes down, he lacked stimulation at home.)

The task is to present the child's point of view, sensitively and without blaming anyone, to the parents and teachers who deal with him everyday. They need to know how it is with him so they don't attach labels or make self-fulfilling negative prophecies.

We find this child exhibits the following major characteristics:

- —an orientation to the present
- —absence of ulterior motives
- —perception of self as a person to whom things happen
- —the absence of a "causative" self.
- —an inability to articulate his point of view; he figures everyone's point of view is the same as his, and
- —he finds us as puzzling as we find him.

Reason for Referral

This child is identified by his teacher who refers him for psychological testing. The teacher states:

Richard is slow in his work. He gets easily sidetracked and likes to clown around. His difficulty is in reading. He is rather heavy and thus a little awkward and his coordination is lacking. However, I do *not* feel he is EMH material. He has ability; he just needs to settle down and learn to apply himself.

Vincent is far behind academically, socially immature, hyperactive, and cannot concentrate on a particular task for more than a few seconds. He has had these troubles ever since he started school. He has never been held back even though it was often recommended that he be retained. He can do pretty well if just the two of us work together and there are no interruptions, but in the group situation he can't get anything done. He can focus his attention if you touch him, but if you just tell him what to do he doesn't seem to understand. He has lots of information and can tell you about it, but he can't get it down in writing. He is becoming more and more of a behavior problem as he becomes more and more frustrated. It is difficult to assign him work that he is able to do because he says, "That's for babies."

Jerry does annoying things that make other children dislike sitting near him. He mutters to himself, plays with gadgets, and is restless and unsettled. He seems insensitive to the fact he is making himself unpopular and he doesn't care. He is not especially disobedient, just heedless. He is extremely irreponsible but has never been defiant or refused to do a job. He just lets it slide.

Mark is a likeable, cooperative, easily flustered, often confused and seldom attentive fifth-grade boy. In general school activities, his academic and growing social problems are most evident. In most of his academic subjects, Mark is working at a grade level below his present fifth-grade placement. He has trouble concentrating. He misses explanations and instructions even though he is physically in the classroom when they are given. His growing social problems also stem from the fact that he just doesn't know what is going on. He sits in his seat while his whole row gets up and gets into line; at recess he ran the wrong way in the football game; in health class the day's discussion was about dentists and he proceeded to start a story about a trip he made to the doctor. He does strange things which seem to indicate that he just isn't tuned in to what is going on around him.

Randy is a discipline problem. He has no respect for others. He hits, shoves, teases, and takes things that belong to his classmates. He insists upon being first. He will not accept being wrong and pouts or has a tantrum when corrected. He threatens other kids to give him things and when he is angry he threatens to fight on the way home. If the lesson appeals to him, he hurries through it making careless mistakes. At other times he is drawing pictures, playing with pencils or causing a disturbance. I need help.

John's problems are mainly academic, some social. He is in the fourth grade and he reads at high second-grade level. His attack on words is fairly adequate if given long enough time to ponder them. It takes John quite a long time to complete any work. He is quite accurate if not hurried. John's number concepts are also behind grade level. He has not displayed a lot of creative ability in school work, he is generally a follower in activities. He has one main friend who is the leader and John is the follower. They have been close friends since preschool. He has been participating well in gym class, but he seldom contributes to classroom group discussions. His mind wanders from the subject frequently. When I ask him a question in class, one which he should be able to answer with no trouble, he will usually roll his eyes or stare at the ceiling looking like he's thinking, but he doesn't give an answer.

A Bow to Tradition

And so, the child is seen for psychological testing. He is given the following tests:

Wechsler Intelligence Scale for Children
Bender-Visual-Motor Gestalt Test
Wide Range Achievement Test
Illinois Test of Psycholinguistic Ability
Benton Visual-Retention Test
Wepman Auditory Discrimination Test
House-Tree-Person Test
Peabody Picture Vocabulary Test
Children's Apperception Test

. . . and all these numerical scores and results magically *become* this child and the task is to make sense out of the test results—a step removed (maybe a mile-high step) from the child.

This seems to be so for on many occasions a fellow psychologist says to you, "Take a look at this kid," and he hands you a folder with a sheaf of papers. They think you're being smart or nit-picking when you say, "That's not a kid, that's a folder and a sheaf of papers." Well, so we're all maybe victims of our training. It takes some of us years to overcome the *shoulds* and *oughts* of the professional role and we continue tradition blindly.

You look at the data and try to answer nonsense questions like, "Is he emotionally disturbed or is he learning disabled?" You feel like calling your colleague on the phone and saying, "He's learning disabled," wait a week, call him back and say, "Hey, I was wrong, he's emotionally disturbed." After another week call back and ask, "Is he any better? Does knowing make a difference?"

Back to test results and looking at all the fragments and pieces: "What would you say his intelligence is from looking at his Bender-Gestalt?" You suspect it's a trap, but you say, "I.Q. is 76½." They say "NIGYYSOB, it's 103 on the Stanford-Binet!"

or

"He drew a square around each Bender design. Do you agree with the Wichita people that this is emotional disturbance?"

or

"What do you make of the single line of smoke from the chimney?" You guess, "Maybe there's warmth in his house??"—Nope—"It means he wets the bed."

or

"Look at this house!" (It's a very empty house. His try at perspective results in a lop-sided box with a diagonal attempt that steps wavering to nowhere. Seems incomplete.) "He's emotionally disturbed! !"

You see, it's not exactly the test data that determines a nonsense diagnosis. The tester has a lot of "Background Information" that supports "Emotional Disturbance" so you try a new tack:

"Did he *seem* emotionally disturbed when you tested him?"
"Whaddaya mean?"
"Did he seem nervous or anxious with you?"
"No—it was like he'd known me all of his life."
"Was he friendly?"
"Yes."
"Did he seem open or devious?"
"Well, he *seemed* open."
"Did he smile?"
"Yes—sometimes he'd smile to cover-up when he didn't know an
     answer."
"How do you know his motivation?"
"The teacher says he cons her all the time."
"Did you feel he was conning you?"
"No—that's what makes him such a good conner."
"How do you account for the lack of any overt symptoms of emo-
     tional disturbance?"
"He has a core of anxiety and anger which is repressed."

So, refer the repressed core and leave the kid alone.

Most of us look at the kid and say, "If I behaved the way he behaves, my motivations would be *(fill in the blanks)*." That's why he looks different to each of us: his behavior is in accordance with the situation and it's his very lack of a core that allows us to write our own history on his magic slate.

We spend all our time looking *inside* him and not enough time looking at the situations in which he functions or disfunctions.

But, we must return to the teacher who has referred him. We have examined, and we are ready to have a case conference to "share test results and make recommendations." Remember—this teacher has tried everything and nothing has worked. He takes all her time. She feels like a failure. So, we come in and say things about Oedipal and I.Q., unconscious motivation, input and output, sib rivalry generalized to peer group, over- or under-protection, denial and defensiveness, numbers, percentile rank, grade equivalents, and lots about

    a) his having it too hard at home
    b) his having it too easy at home

and we make a list of twenty more things for her to try, to this teacher we do this, and she has several ways to react:

    a) "My God, is there no end to it? I'm really a failure."
    b) Her eyes roll up and sideways as she pretends it makes sense so we don't feel too badly.
    c) "I knew he couldn't read—now I know why."
    d) "So it's the parent's fault, not mine."
    e) "It's only November—school's not out until June!"
    f) "He's too complicated for me—are *you* gonna treat him?"
    g) "With all this to do, I'd better not refer the other three!"

There are some ways to do an evaluation to make it more meaningful and sometimes more helpful: Is it really reasonable for a psychologist to think that he knows more about a child after being with him for two hours (or even four) than a teacher who has had him in class? Or more than the parents who have had him a lifetime? Is it reasonable to assume the test situation elicits conclusions that generalize to classroom or home? Is it reasonable to look only inside the child for explanations of behavioral clashes that occur between or among people?

Maybe a place to start is to recognize that observations made by parents and teachers provide more central data than do tests. (Or just read the social history at the Mental Health Center.) Major diagnostic clues are contained in referral statements like the following:

    We've tried everything and nothing works.
    He is so irresponsible.
    He is very disorganized.
    He wants *all* my attention.
    When you have him alone, you couldn't ask for a nicer child.
    He could do it if he wanted to.
    He can't get along with his peers; he does better with younger or
        older kids.

He tends to be a loner.
He's not withdrawn, but he's always alone.
He's different.
Rules don't seem to apply to him.
Time means nothing to him.
He sits and does nothing.
He forgets.
He wants everything he sees.
He doesn't hold a grudge.
He doesn't stick with anything.
He's a good worker, if you tell him exactly what to do.
He wants to *do* things . . . but not school work.
He always has to be first.
He doesn't seem to feel guilty.
He loves animals.
It's hard for him to make a choice.
He can't get started; he doesn't finish things.
He doesn't seem to feel pain the way the others do.
He makes promises, but doesn't carry them through.
No, he doesn't seem to be unhappy.
He's open and honest, but he lies and sometimes he steals.
He's selfish, yet he's generous.
Function is determined by complexity of the situation.
He's a good salesman.
He never met a stranger.
He has a problem I can't cope with because I can't name it.

Maybe psychological tests can be more useful if they are not secret, magic procedures that only you know about. Try letting the parents or teacher observe as you test and explain in asides as the kid gives you leads. Write your report so anyone can read it without feeling bad. Leave off the "Confidential" stamp and leave out the negative labels. For example:

PSYCHOLOGICAL REPORT

Reason for Referral:

Clarence was referred by his teacher who describes him as having the characteristics of a child with learning disabilities. "In his behavior pattern he has a short attention span, is easily distracted, his body is in constant motion, and he is unable to remain at one task for any length of time. With his motor facilitation he is poorly coordinated and has balance difficulty. He exhibits difficulty with rhythms and directions (left and right). He does average work in oral reading and doesn't appear to have any difficulty with eye movement or head jerking although he constantly loses his place. He has managed to work at the level with his group all this year, but continues to make many numerals and letters in reverse. He holds a pencil or chalk very tightly and the lines appear shaky, heavy, and uneven. Other than making his numerals in reverse Clarence has managed to stay with the group in math although it takes him forever to complete any exercise compared to any other child. He is not a sought-after child and is frequently alone on the playground. In a kindergarten sociogram he was not chosen as a friend by any children in the group of twenty-five.

In what areas may the parents and I help Clarence? Will there be a classroom for perceptually handicapped children that he could attend?

Background Information:

Clarence resides with his mother and father, a sister who is eight years old and a sister who is four and one-half years old. It is noted that Clarence did not crawl as a baby, but pulled his body when on his hands and knees. When he began walking, his coordination was very poor and he fell frequently. (On the day of testing he had a large skinned mark on his forehead as a result of having fallen.) The teacher had recommended swimming as an aid to his coordination. The parents are very cooperative and very aware of Clarence's difficulties and want to be as helpful as possible to him.

Clarence is younger than most other children in the class having started to school at age four years and eleven months. His attendance is regular and he is said to achieve at an average level in reading and arithmetic although his handwriting is described as poor. There is no history of speech problems.

Vision and hearing were checked by the school nurse. The test findings are recorded as satisfactory. Birth followed after four hours of labor, no drugs or instruments were used. His birth condition is described as good; he was not premature; his birthweight was seven pounds and his color is described as good. There were no known birth injuries and it is stated that he breathed easily. Developmental milestones—walking eleven months, words other than *mama* or *dada* at age sixteen months, and he combined words at age twenty-four months. There were no feeding problems. Bowel training began at twenty-four months and was completed at age three years. He was dry day and night at age five years though he still wets the bed occasionally.

He had chicken pox at age four years and it is described as having been a light case. There was an ear infection in January of this year when he had a cold. He has never had a high temperature and his general health has always been very good, according to his mother. The mother states that Clarence was a very fat baby and his coordination was always very poor in that he fell frequently and always had a bruise on his forehead. There were six stitches taken at one time, but no concussions. The school nurse states that the mother agrees with the teacher that he is hyperactive and adds that the mother feels that he has a "middle-child syndrome."

The mother is a nurse and works two nights a week. His older sister is described as very quiet and the mother states that all three children transpose syllables of words in general conversation as well as when reading. The mother is described as a very relaxed person who is not overly concerned about Clarence and who realistically expects age to solve some of his problems.

Previous Psychological Test Results:

Clarence was administered the Primary Mental Abilities Test when he was five years and seven months old and achieved an I.Q. of 122 on this group-administered test. There is no record of any other psychological testing.

Present Psychological Test Results:

Wechsler Intelligence Scale for Children
                  Verbal I.Q.   109
                  Performance I.Q.   115
                  Full Scale I.Q.   113

Draw-A-Man Test
                  Drawing I.Q.   155

Analysis of Results:

Clarence was accompanied by his parents to the testing session. They stayed and observed and learned.

Intellectual functioning is at a bright normal level. Clarence displays much better ability in mastering materials and ideas presented visually than he does ideas and information presented auditorily. When visual cues are added to the auditory instructions, performance is much improved. Clarence relates easily and well and gives no indications of emotional disturbance.

The source of his hyperactivity is pretty clearly situational in that in the more complex situation of the classroom he has considerably more difficulty in staying organized and focused on a task. In the one-to-one relationship where structure and organization can be provided as needed, he functions quite adequately. It was necessary on occasion to point to where he was to begin and it is obvious that there are many times when he cannot sequence events automatically but needs help in this area. When he is asked a question to which he does not have a ready answer, he closes his eyes, squeezes his hands against his head, and frowns. He does not say, "I don't know," but maintains this attitude until encouraged to go on to the next question or until he is given an additional cue which would help him to formulate a response.

He tends to whisper instructions to himself as he performs visual-motor tasks and he seems to find this helpful in terms of maintaining organization. There are many times when he is not sure whether or not he is finished with a task and has real difficulty sorting out the beginning, the middle, and the end of both visually and auditorily presented materials.

Sensory integration required in the performance of written work, for example, is quite difficult for him to achieve and maintain. He needs to work "larger"—for example, at the blackboard, to assist him in achieving integration.

The high pain threshold which is so common to many children with this kind of difficulty is reported by the parents to be the case with Clarence. In addition, the self is experienced rather passively—things "happen to" him—rather than his experiencing himself as an active doer whose actions have a cause relationship with resulting events. Just as he shows difficulty with effectively sequencing events in time, he shows difficulty in predicting consequences of actions and activities. This is related to his orientation which is mostly in terms of the present and contributes to the parents' puzzlement at his tendency to repeat actions or acts for which he has been punished in the past. He does not connect punishment in the past with the present situation and tends to live each moment "fresh"—he forgives easily—(he has no past)—and since he does not carry over the past into the present, does not experience guilt with the intensity that others do.

This boy displays many of the classic symptoms of hyperactivity and disorganization which frequently respond well to medication and it has been suggested to the parents that they consult with their pediatrician concerning the possibilities for using medication on a trial basis.

The parents are interested, cooperative, and warm people who have very positive feelings both for Clarence and the school which he attends. They are especially appreciative of the assistance and cooperation which Clarence's teacher has given them. They expressed appreciation to the teacher and the principal for referring Clarence for evaluation and can be counted on to carry through on recommendations.

The referral materials prepared by Clarence's teacher and by the school nurse were exceptionally well done. The excellent behavioral observations and the inclusion of examples were very helpful.

A case conference with school personnel will be held in the near future and a copy of this report is to be sent to the pediatrician as requested by the parents.

Inside Russell Gene

Go to a case conference to share information so recommendations come from the group. Self-imposed ideas are more likely followed through than recommendations based on your psychological role.

Parents and teachers have made all the observations. We help them put it together and encourage them to have confidence in what they observe.

There are different ways to share information. The following material resulted when the teacher referred Russell Gene for a psychological evaluation. The case conference was attended by his mother, his teachers, his school nurse, his principal and the school psychologist.

Russell is repeating the first grade. He is referred by his teacher who describes him as having difficulty in the academic, social, emotional and behavioral areas. Russell is the youngest of four children having two sisters and a brother older. The school nurse speculates that the sisters have babied him, kept him dependent far too long. The mother speculates that she has done the same thing and reasons that part of this is because she has to work and doesn't have time to wait for him to get dressed in the morning. He only learned to tie his shoes a couple of weeks ago, and he is seven years old. She is critical of herself for this but she adds, "If I don't dress him he puts his shirt on backwards, or he'll put his shoes on and then he can't get his pants on . . . or he gets completely dressed and I discover that he hasn't even put his shorts on." It's a hassle for her to get to work in the morning and she has to rush him. She finally gets him up and down to the breakfast table. He pours milk on his cereal, and sometimes gets up and forgets to eat it. He goes off to school without his lunch money, and then forgets that he forgot his lunch money and goes to the cafeteria before he remembers that he doesn't have any money to pay for his lunch. The mother makes a good case for the boy having emotional problems. She suggests that it is her fault and the fault of her older daughters who cater to him.

86

He *does* have trouble in the academic, social, emotional, and behavioral areas. His teachers say, "Most of the time he is happy and unconcerned about his behavior. He seems to know what is expected, but makes no effort to remember. He is absent-minded, as if his thoughts are far off. He constantly makes noises and is moving most of the time. He interrupts. He cannot wait his turn. He cannot concentrate and this affects his learning. His feelings are easily hurt when he is corrected, but he forgets it in a few minutes and often repeats what he was corrected for. He has to be urged to complete assignments. He even has to be told to blow his nose all the time. The reason for referral is to learn how we can best help this child, and also how this child can learn to help himself.

The school nurse reports that hearing and vision are OK, and the physician has marked every item normal on the school physical report. Birth history—normal. He walked later than the other children—didn't even try until he was fourteen months old. Never had any feeding problems. He still wets the bed occasionally. They say he has always been well. The school nurse says, "The parents are aware that he has had too many tasks done for him by his sisters. They feel that they have not given him the chances to do and learn for himself. They are anxious for any help available."

On psychological evaluation Russell Gene measures low-average intelligence. He functions academically quite a bit below what you would predict on the basis of his intelligence. He confided that he didn't talk in school the same way he talked to the psychologist. He said that he pays attention to the other kids instead of to the teacher.

There were many reversals. He spelled the word *Go H-e-f*. He was able to make the individual sounds of the letters of a word but he couldn't put them together. For example, he sounded out the word *book*, *b-o-k*, and then said, "Oh *curve*, it says curve." He sounded out EAT and said "Crane." He was very talkative. Bender-Gestalt showed considerable difficulty in visual integration. He couldn't organize the parts into a visual whole. As he printed his name he whispered the letters to himself. It was a very labored performance. Most tasks he worked very fast; his mouth was always moving; he would whisper to himself as he was trying to draw and write, "Wait!" or "There!" He whispered directions to his pencil, "Go over, go down, there." Frequently he would lose his place in the task. He would stop and talk and forget where he was or that he was even engaged in a task. When he was making lines, he would use a right-to-left sequence rather than left-to-right. He engaged in a lot of word-hunting when he was asked a question that required a specific answer. On questions that could be answered in many different ways he did very well. Vocabulary is average for his age. On the picture arrange-

ment subtest he found the numbers and letters on the back of the cards
and used them to arrange the sequence and then said that he was peek-
ing. Once in a while he would say, "I'm smart, ain't I?" He got very
tired and restless. He asked questions like, "How much did your desk
cost? How much did your chair cost?" When asked his three wishes, he
said, "Not to go to school, a thousand dollars, a pet lion and a dog."
He said that his pet turtle got run over and his sister ran out and saved
the shell. She saved the wrong part—he would have saved the turtle!

That was the information you had at the time of the conference with
teachers, parents, principal, school nurse, and psychologist. So how did
the conference go?

The teachers came in and they saw the mother there; their lips
tightened a little. They had been looking for a chance to say how it was
with this boy, and they felt they wouldn't be able to really say . . . with
the mother present. We started by asking the mother to tell a little bit
about how it was with Russell at home. She said she really gets upset
with him. She has to tell him to do something three or four times. He
seems to be off in another world. He acts like he doesn't hear. He
watches only cartoons on television, nothing else. He is always into
things; doesn't pick up his toys, won't clean up his room. When he brings
homework home and he is supposed to study, he never gets to it. If she
tries to help him and he makes mistakes he gets real mad and he quits
trying. She said, "He can never sit still. He is always on the move, and
he even forgets to eat sometimes." She says she figures it is probably her
fault. She dresses him, she gets impatient with him, she has to get to
work. She has to pry him out of bed in the morning, and he won't even
put his clothes on unless she gets them and lays them out for him. If he
dresses himself, he asks her which foot the shoes go on. She tells him,
"Put them on and if they hurt you got them on the wrong feet." But he
doesn't hurt. He puts them on the wrong feet and they feel OK to him.
She gets so mad at him that she whips him. "He doesn't cry, he just looks
at me. When one of the girls is teasing him, he can *pretend* that he is
hurt and he raises a big scene, but when he is really hurt he acts like it
doesn't hurt." She said that she can't figure him out.

One of the teachers shared how it was with him: "Well, he mainly
does what he wants to do. He talks all the time, he doesn't follow
through, he has his arm in the air making noises like an airplane, and
when I ask him to stop he acts surprised as if he didn't know what he was
doing. I set him next to me—and most children when I set them next to
me they don't dare misbehave because they are afraid—but he's not
scared of me and he goes on and does his stuff anyhow." The teachers
say that he is very difficult to control. That he's got something going all

the time. They can't teach him anything, they can't get his attention, and they have trouble teaching any of the other children anything. They set him on a chair in the back of the room, and then he goes home and tells his mother—then she's been calling the principal and getting mad at him because she figures that her boy has been mistreated.

What happens when you get the parents and teachers and everyone concerned together in the same conference is that you get a bigger picture of the boy's behavior. You see the same factors operating in both the home situation and the school situation. It eliminates the tendency for parent to blame the school and school to blame the parent, and you are able to focus more immediately upon the real task of being some assistance to this child, and some assistance to the teacher.

You could make a good case for this boy's being emotionally disturbed. Certainly there seem to be enough factors in the background that would suggest that. The parents having been separated, there is a lot of difficulty going on in the home, and this is a working mother. He is the youngest, the baby, and maybe he is the scapegoat for all the problems. You could formulate it that way, except that this is not a tense child. He does not seem to be disturbed. His teachers seem to be disturbed, and his mother seems to be disturbed, but *he* does not seem to be disturbed.

You can certainly present Russell Gene as a NOW child. He lives mostly in the present—with very little awareness of the past or the future. A lot of things they said would make it seem so: "I'm really mad at him, I chew him out. He feels bad for just a few moments, and then he is over it, smiling and relating to me, as if nothing happened. He promises not to do it again, but he's at it and doing it again as if he is not even aware that he is doing it. He seems genuinely puzzled when I call it to his attention."

He is the kind of a child who experiences life as *happening to* him, from moment to moment, and does not see his part in making events occur. He does not see his part in generating the angry feedback that he gets from people. And he really is puzzled by it. Most of the time he does seem happy, and unconcerned. It is very obvious that he cannot sequence events in a time dimension. He can't even sequence the order in which he puts his clothes on every morning, much less the various steps by which he will arrive at a solution to an arithmetic problem. He can't integrate elements into a whole, either visual or auditory: for example, sounding out the individual sounds of a word.

He quits in the middle of a task, but he doesn't even know that he's in the middle. Sometimes he doesn't even start a task because he doesn't know *where* to start. There is some evidence to suggest that if he knows where to begin and where to end and what goes in-between, if he knows the steps, then he sticks to a task and does a good job. He always has to be first. He can't take turns because taking turns again is sequencing events in a time dimension. He has to be first for now is all there is—for him there isn't a later. His mother describes him as a boy who loses everything. He has lost six pair of gloves this year. If he wears his coat to school and if it warms up when school is out, he leaves his coat at school. He never remembers that he is going to need it tomorrow. He doesn't even remember to stay mad. He has no ulterior motives. He is just what you see at the moment. He doesn't do this to bug you because he can't plan ahead for that kind of a goal.

What you try to modify are the attitudes and labels that they put on this boy. And you try to explain why it is that he seems much better when you have him alone than when he is in a group. You get them to observe that he uses the same techniques in the group that he does when he's with you alone. But these techniques in the group do not take into consideration the needs of the other children in the group. He doesn't have the ability to modify his behavior as a function of awareness of needs of others. He seems to be thinking of himself all the time.

He whispers directions to himself to help him stay organized, and that is what the teacher sees as "muttering" to himself. He is very disorganized. He can't get his paper and pencil out to start a task. His desk is always an awful mess. Can never find anything. Seems to need more room to work.

He's up and around with his elbows flying and . . . most of all he needs to stay unlabeled so he can make progress. He seems very complicated because he is so simple. He is just what you see at the moment. Teachers and parents try to guess what his motivation is from his behavior. You can't do it unless you know how it is with him—*for he is very unlike you.*

You need to be as direct with him as he is with you. You need to apply structure to the point where he *does* know what comes next, where it is possible for him to perform and learn. He is not able to play social games with you; subtleties, sarcasm, innuendoes are wasted on him. He responds only to the direct message. The teachers come to realize that if they want him to do something, they have to tell him to do it *now* . . . for he has no later. But he does have a present, and he's willing to please.

We talked about giving him his own "office," as a way of cutting down distraction, as a way of helping him to keep structured. But to put him in there, period, is very little help unless they also get him started . . . with a smaller assignment, one that he can handle, to "point" him. If you give him the same assignment that everyone else has been given, and then simply put him in the walled-up space, it really is very little help to him. We talked about making arrows in the blanks to show him where to go next on paper, and about the need to have more space around problems because he writes bigger, messier.

Is there anything he does well? He talks well. Can they use that in a productive, positive way? He talks all the time. How can they turn it off? If they can give him a task, and get him hooked into it so he can do it. It's when he gets lost that he starts talking, and he says whatever comes into his head . . . "How much does your desk cost?"

The teachers raised the question of whether some of the other children might be of help to him, instead of only the teacher herself. She has all the rest of the children to take care of. She thought she might sit him next to an organized child so he could see what the sequence is, when he should get the paper and pencil out, etc. The teacher said, "Well, he doesn't need any instruction in how to copy!" That indicates that he *does* want to do well. Can they change their attitude about the nastiness of copying . . . as something bad that he should not be permitted to do, but rather as something he should be encouraged to do appropriately.

Something has to be said about the *tone* of this conference. Teachers come; they are getting together to talk about this boy. They come feeling angry and frustrated. They've had it with this kid; they've tried everything, and it would be a relief to have the opportunity to share with each other, to tell somebody how bad it is with maybe the possibility that he might be taken out of the class and put somewhere else. When they first come, it isn't so much a matter of "Help us" because they don't feel that anything can be done. Haven't they tried?!?

They walk in and they see the parent sitting there. They didn't get the message that she was going to be there. That isn't the way conferences had been held. At first there is the feeling of disappointment. It is not going to be the way they planned. They are not going to be able to say what is on their minds and in their hearts because you can't say those things in front of the mother. They get tense. Who is going to blame them? They might be accused of not doing a good job—they are failures as teachers. They already feel this within themselves and that's bad enough. They don't need to be told.

Then something unexpected happens. The meeting is conducted in such a way that the mother begins talking—"Tell me how it is with Russell Gene at home." They hear her say that she has the very same troubles at home that the teachers have at school. She is worried, she feels angry and frustrated—in the same way that they are angry and frustrated—and it is as if everyone surprisingly has the same feelings about this child. She also has had it. Then you get the bigger picture because what she experiences at home is almost identical to what the teachers experience in the classroom.

Teachers mainly think that parents will never admit that their child behaves badly, is difficult to live with. And in these situations this is often the first thing the parents talk about. They don't say that reading is poor and spelling, too; that the child is getting low grades. If given a chance, they tend to tell how it is in terms of how difficult it is to live with him. The teacher learns immediately that it is *not* just that he cannot start with one and go through ten arithmetic problems. He can't start and get dressed in the morning. He can't sequence the order in which his clothes go on his body. That's easier for her to understand so she gains new insights. He can't follow the directions which all the other children seem to get quite easily. She gives the assignment to everyone else in the class and they go ahead and do it. It's only when she goes away that he *won't* do it by himself. He could if he wanted to! The point is that he *can't*. And she has to know that he can't.

The same thing happens with the mother. She says, "He can't get going." "He never gets dressed." You ask, "What happens if you help him?" "Oh, then there is no problem, but I have to start sometime teaching him to do these things by himself. He is eight years old, you know. It's not that's he's four or five."

She continues, "He forgot the way to go home one night. He went to the wrong house. The lady called me up (I had been worried sick when he didn't come home): 'I got your little boy over here. He doesn't know the way home.' 'But,' I sputtered to myself, 'he has walked home dozens of times.' I get so mad at him I'm afraid to whip him . . . I'm afraid I'd kill him."

And when teachers hear a mother say this, they feel for the mother because they have felt the same thing themselves.

The meeting cannot end there. They are saying, "So, this is the way it is, but we don't understand it. How can he walk home and do it very well sometimes, and then one day he doesn't get there at all? It's the inconsistency. He looks better than he seems to be. We've tried everything and it doesn't work. He is so perplexing." If they could understand, it wouldn't be so bad. But they don't. And not only that, but he takes up all their time. He doesn't seem to learn and he makes them feel like failures. He is so disruptive that they cannot teach the rest of the class. They are worn out at the end of the day. Mother says, "I also am worn out." But she accuses herself of having given him a wrong start. What's the matter with this boy? That's still the main question. What's going on with him?

That's where you step in. The parents and teachers have provided all the information and then you give the interpretation by using all the

given material. You might say, "Nobody is going to argue with you—
we all know how it is. We've all lived with him. What makes him tick?"
And then you begin to explain to them how it is.

"I'm going to tell you what it is like inside Russell Gene. I'm going to
tell you how he sees the world. And I think it is going to make a
difference in how you see him."

You give organization to all this apparently unrelated data. You pull
it together in such a way so they can say, "Aha, so that's the way it is."
And then they add and embroider; offer more anecdotes, their own
illustrative material. And when they do that, you know they truly understand what's going on. Then the anger disappears; they don't have to be
angry anymore. There's no fight against it . . . it simply dissolves. He's
not seen as angry. That's what has been so puzzling. They no longer see
him as someone trying to make them look bad. The parents and teachers
say, "OK, we understand," which means, "We don't feel so bad about
him any more." What do we do about it? How do we help him? You tell
them, "If you can see the world from his point of view, then you know
how it is with him and what you have to do to make it possible for him
to be successful." Then you have to get them to give some examples.
You can't let them leave right then.

It may be obvious to you (making the application) but it is not
obvious to them. Questions need to be asked, such as . . . "What do you
do with him now?" The teacher reports, "I set him in the corner on a
chair. I have to because he disrupts the whole class." (She has to consider her needs and the needs of the class. That's the most important
thing you can say first!) There are times when he goes into orbit when
he *does* have to be contained. Instead of setting him back in that corner
as punishment, put him there until he can get reorganized, and maybe
even give him a structured task to do that has a beginning, a middle, and
an end. Something you know he can do. He comes to appreciate the
opportunity to get reorganized. And he quits seeing it as punishment.

That's the kind of illustrative material that you give. You get the
teachers to say what they do already; the same with the mother. Suggest
that they do much the same thing with a different motivation, different
goals in mind, taking into consideration his needs, rather than their anger.
If parents and teachers can see it from his point of view then they can
do what's needed more positively and more objectively, without all the
strain and worry and anger that wears them out.

What does he do best? He has to be the first one up to erase the
chalkboard. If there is a message to be taken to the principal's office and
he knows the way, he wants to do that. Yeah, but then the teachers says,
"If I give him those jobs to do all the time I'm in trouble with the rest
of my class because they think I favor him . . . and besides, they want a

chance to do it, too." The teacher says, "I really don't understand him. Like tonight, when we leave the room we put the chairs on the desks. He was putting the chairs on the desks of the children who were absent. Of course, all the rest of us were waiting on him. But sometimes in that way he is very helpful."

What it is also pointing out, and mothers say it all the time, is this: "The things I need to do for him that are helpful, take *time!*" This mother said, "Instead of hollering at him through the door in the morning, I'm not going to be as angry with him. I'm going to go in and get him up. Instead of ranting at him to get dressed, I'm going to lay out his clothes for him in the order that he puts them on . . . first, instead of last, like I've been doing."

Mothers have to face the question they fear: "Is it *all right* for me to help him when he is eight years old, or ten, the way I would have when he was four or five? I didn't mind then, but don't I have to begin sometime to teach him how to do it by himself?" Parents have to consider the choice. If he doesn't function and can't get going on his own, but can do much better if you help him to get started, you have to help him . . . but you have to feel that it is all right. It's not that he won't . . . not that he can and won't. He can't. That's what they have to know.

So we understand all that, but what can we do about it. We're on the same side, but how does that help?

> —If you don't take credit for his behavior by accepting blame, perhaps you can start giving him credit with positive you-did-its!
>
> —You do what you do more comfortably, because at this point in time he needs it—not because he is conning you.
>
> —Know that he *does* change—slowly up to now—but sometimes, when pressure comes off, sometimes there's a great leap of integration and you can shout inside, "My God! HE DID IT!" Out loud you say, "That makes *you* feel good," as you share pleasure with him.

It's hard to say how it happens—for example, the mother has been griping about the reading teacher and the boy has, too. Too much pressure, too many standards he can't meet, too little progress. He's still stuck on the brown level in the SRA materials—and in the meeting the mother gets an "Aha!" when she sees that what she dislikes in the teacher is that she acts like herself!

So each forgives each and knows—sometimes you get sore. You want him to succeed. But you also learn that *your* success does not depend upon him so you drive a little less and guide a little more.

The teacher who has said to you in private, "I think the mother does too much for him," or "He is alone too much at home and gets no direction," gets a chance to check it out with the mother directly. (She discovers things going on—worries, concerns she didn't even dream of.) And she knows parents are interested because they are there.

"It's easier to try again tomorrow if I know it's not all my fault."

"Obviously his assignments need to be shorter, and I'm sending less homework. No use your suffering, too."

"Listen—he's *not* unhappy. I don't know why—Lord knows I'd be depressed if treated the way I treat him!"

And some mothers cry with relief because they may get some help from teachers and principals who assist without blame.

You *could* formulate it:

"He's the youngest in a family of four kids. He has three older siblings who cater to his every need. He didn't even have to learn to talk as early as other kids because he got what he wanted just by grunting. The parents have been separated, this is a working mother. This child has been overprotected and neglected. They haven't taken the time to teach him anything. He comes to school totally unprepared. He didn't even learn to tie his shoes until two weeks ago. Lazy. Thinks only of himself. And the father blames the mother. *He* doesn't have that trouble with him. She says it's *his* fault. The boy is just like him. He had to go to a special class when he was a kid. This mother is terribly worried that the boy will turn out like his uncle. The boy is a scapegoat in that family. He's the one that keeps the rest of them free from pathology."

You can make a case like that. "Very severe oedipal," "identification problem," "sexual role reversal," "anxiety reaction, other," "over-protective mother," "acts out the father's unconscious," etc.

But if you do, where do you go from there, after you've blamed someone?

At the end of the conference the mother volunteered that she could send him to a church school where classes were four or five to a class, where one of the teachers, a minister's wife, loved him because he was the age of a daughter she'd lost, and if this had been suggested just an hour earlier, reactions would perhaps have been different. But now, with some new understanding . . .

Principal:	"We know how it is with him. Let's get that refrigerator carton and build him his own office."
Teacher:	"Let's try him the rest of the year."
School Nurse:	"Let me contact the family physician; maybe medication would help."

When you've invested so much in a child, even if it has been negative, you rather want to see how it comes out when there are new things to try—especially if they are your ideas and they haven't been forced on you by some external expert. The feeling is one of group concern about a little boy that everyone likes.

Rickadalco and Fewnephize Four

Learning disability or teaching disability?

As is traditional in this nation of rugged individuals we look inside the person for the wrong "things" which will account for "wrong" functioning.

We teach them as a group but blame them individually. They don't fit, they don't belong. I teach him but he refuses to *learn*.

Someone once compared schools to a race: everyone starts at go and runs for nine months. Some finish the race, some are only one-half or three-fourths of the way around the track when the signal sounds for the beginning of a *new* race.

Well, is it learning disability or teaching disability? Who is refereeing the crazy race? Do the runners choose the race? Or their track shoes? Are there relays or rests?

When everyone does the same thing, competing with each other, learning to avoid the bloody lashes symbolized by the red checkmarks, (you're *wrong* you stupid kid, *bleed*), it indeed becomes something less than a humanizing experience. Learn through suffering, and the big problem is he *refuses* even to suffer, which is the only decent thing to do if you don't learn when I teach.

When the teacher's words are not understood, the child hears something like this: "Everyone get out your rickadalco and fewnephize four. George, pay attention! Rickadalco and fewnephize four *now*! Quit whispering to John and get busy *this* minute. Don't *talk*. Raise your hand and I'll get to you as soon as I can. My God, he's seven years old and can't even rickadalco or fewnephize four!" (Poor boy, probably doesn't get enough fewnephizing at home.)

Learning disability is a social judgment made when a child fails to meet performance standards when exposed to a standarized program as a member of a group whose only commonality may be that they've been around approximately the same number of years.

When you teach children all the same, they stay grouped. The individual stays meshed in the mass. And if he emerges, he's often pushed back with a negative "You did it!" His search for connection between self and task is seen through the assumption, "He wants all my attention." He needs remediation—compared to the group. Remediation becomes cure of a lack inside him and the shenanigans in the three-ring learning disability circus keep thousands employed.

The elimination of trial and error learning is made almost permanent by virtue of the fact that children enter school. One can no longer make mistakes and use them to advantage. Errors are cause for laughter from classmates or are circled in red or highlighted by checkmarks.

The emphasis is on "mistakes," and mistakes are *bad* to make. A mistake can no longer serve as a "trial" that did not work from which one learns comfortably. A mistake means one was caught being bad— doing it the wrong way—and the idea is planted that there is only one "right" way. Task approach is narrow and doubly hard—not only to reach the goal, but to avoid any errors along the way. No longer can one comfortably "try something and see if it works" or "see how it fits."

There is no longer practice outside of the formal situation—the play of guessing at letters and words—even of comfortably modeling the behavior of parents—if they are "working" at reading or writing.

Joy flies away like last summer's butterflys and one is left alone and cold waiting to be driven toward goals set by adults. Even one's evaluative attitude toward one's own productions is shattered as "correct" evaluations are made by the teacher. One's self-respect is sorely tried daily and one never really knows what will be evaluated "wrong." (Every little thing counts.)

You no longer learn for the internal feeling of joy as one's performance matches one's own goal, nor can you explore, run toward and away, or sideways and up and down.

Your spirit is broken and your pale scarred face joins the group who do not cooperate with each other toward common goals (this is called cheating). You laugh at your neighbor to deny the tension, and happiness stems from your joy that it's not you. Each in his loneliness is pitted against each and you fight for the beauty of nothingness (a paper devoid of red checkmarks) like machines clicking to the directions of their masters and you soon learn some have it and some don't. And even at home you don't read *Boys Life* or the newspaper because "I'm a poor reader, I might make a mistake."

The superior-subordinate model is established forever and you are forced by law to face the judge of your worthiness who stands viewing your timorous self-respect to checkmark its flaws or, worse, to smile tolerantly at your inadequacies.

When you "know," you are eager to show up your classmates, to put them down so that by comparison you are up. It's all "stuck on"—you're directed by others—there is nothing inside you to give you guidance. You forget you ever wanted, and spend all your time guessing what they want, so like a trained seal you can honk a long EEEEEEEEE! !

They assume you won't learn unless you are driven and soon they are right, they make it come true. At home, your parents join with the drivers (parents stay in their ruts; they don't want it for you). They send their children into the shallow end of the same muck of errors in which they were drowning, forgetting that children are smaller and shorter. Not noticing that their children are drowning, being taught to hold their breath, or at best, treading water. And if they do realize it, they throw them lead life jackets of dire prediction and threat.

The children get no practice in:

—setting their own goals
—evaluating their own performance
—finding a number of ways to approach a new problem
—working together
—appreciating differences
—defining a problem out of their own experience

It's no wonder that many are satisfied with "behavior modification" —so that a child acts in accordance with external standards. The un-animated performance becomes the ideal and the behavior to be modi-fied· is counted by occurrence in time. (In a thirty-minute time sample, hands improperly placed below the waist 87 times; thumb inserted in mouth, 126 times; spoke aloud to his neighbor, 2 times.)

It seems a shame to tell teachers the secret of "these kids": that they are immune to the nuances of sarcasm; that they live in the present so to "learn because you will need it later" is useless as a prod. They, more than others, can't see concensus, custom or usage, or convenience as providing any basis for "doing it *this* way."

Their simple, honest directness is the source of their mystery. As others flip-flop in the symbolic world of "as-if," they focus entirely on the world of "right now"—
        now—
              now—
                     now————

It's About Time

In some ways these children seem to be John Locke's blank tablets waiting to be writ and so you write on them and they turn into magic slates—lift the film and it disappears except for some very faint pressure marks. So nothing makes lasting imprints and tradition is ephemeral and you get only faint hints that tradition is appreciated. "This is the first time we've ever eaten supper without the candle lit." You have to wonder then, if memory was a bobble in the flow of sameness and predictability for you, what must it be for them? A point of smooth in the sea of chaos? A *super* bang in a bang-bang world?

You ask; they say "I remember

—Hitting my brother on the head with a hammer.
—Hiding in the cornfield and getting lost.
—Riding after on my tricycle when you forgot me.
—The carnival, the fireworks, an injured pigeon, a hungry dog.
—Screaming and standing on the rat that turned out to be a shoebrush.
—Falling downstairs into darkness—and staying there in silence.
—Riding high on my uncle's shoulders and being tossed in the air."

So memory is composed of peaks of experience looming out of the chaos. The peaks, unconnected, aren't remembered as ordered in time.

So much of the behavior that really bothers people seems to be related to the child's orientation toward the present, his absence of a connected past and his failure to predict consequences in the projected future.

Life is different for many now. There are cultural factors of mobility and disconnectedness affecting larger numbers of children than in the past. Sameness and stability that used to be taken for granted simply do not exist for many today.

Time was noted and punctuated by regularly occurring events—a fixed time for bed, for meals, for a bath. Perception of past and prediction of future was based on this sameness. The sameness served as a predictable given—a base along which limited events could be stretched.

Connections in time are easier for a child born and raised in the same house, in the same town, in the same state—for all of his childhood. Perhaps the routine and regularity partly explains the observation that the incidence of learning disability is lower in rural populations.

Neighborhood play groups were composed of children variant in age. The older ones served as a model of futureness—with traditional roles and privileges connected with age, size, and time. Empathy with the younger is easier if you've been there and one's position in the group was stable and sure.

Today's groupings are same-age mates in separate rooms in separate schools. Models of past and of future are more distant and remote. One's world is more present, competition more pressing, and sameness more valued.

An observation repeatedly made by teachers and parents of Now Children is that they "get along fine with younger children—or with older ones—but not with their classmates." This may reflect the child's search for his place by seeking models of past and of future. Certainly the intensity of competition is reduced—with younger, he leads; with older, he follows—and the niches are wider than positions among peers.

In the past, delay was easier to tolerate because the child knew the day was coming when he'd be old enough or big enough. He could see where he was going and he knew where he'd been. He was a part of a connected stream, with time to become involved in a larger self-history.

Routine was established for larger time units—day, week, month, season, year; and experience closely matched expectation. Cause and effect connections were easier to make when you lived in the same place, in the same way, for a long time. Living in the same house and community over a long period permitted collecting relics of tradition— pictures, furniture, recipes, wedding gown, toys, crocks, iron kettles, quilts and quilt frames, anvils and tools. A child in this setting meshed daily as he handled and did with objects and tools from his past.

Life was not necessarily better—for many, tradition was a terrible trap—but, better or worse, prediction was more stable, position more rooted, and both self and others had durable knowledge concerning appropriateness matched with situation.

Possessions were firmly a part of each person made more durable by repetitive use over a long period of time. Children grew up with the same people, in the same place, with the same things, with relatively extended concept of future.

Have they been with us always, the Now Children? Is identification just better? If you look only at children you will conclude—maybe, yes. But functioning (or mal-functioning) occurs in situations and there is evidence to suggest that situations have changed. The comparison (or competition) group for the child today, is narrower, more changing than groups of the past. The "retarded" have been siphoned out reducing the range. "Tracking" has further tightened the group. The goal is to treat them alike and subjects are taught—not children. To do this, you must have a group that's the same. And in a sea of expected sameness, even wavelets stick out. *He's different!*

That's not the whole story. Children are brought to narrow groups hauled from the visual chewing gum world of T.V. with little knowledge of doing, of searching, of contributing positively. Life happens to them and they participate minimally in determining their destiny. They lack causative self.

Mike is a modern Now Child. Let Mike's mother tell you; this is a letter she wrote to his therapist:

> Mike seems to be living without any limits at all, and I thought it might be helpful if I gave you a run-down on the situation, which I find almost intolerable.
>
> Summer school started Monday. I dropped him off with what I hoped were words of encouragement and told him to make it home by suppertime. He arrived home with friends at 11:30 p.m. to collect some cigarettes he'd stashed in the bushes. Then, they all took off for the Coffee Shop, and he finally came home to stay at 1:55 A.M. So I didn't get him up for school because he didn't get to bed until 3 A.M. Then last night he dropped in with one of his companions for a five-minute dinner and took off until 1 A.M. This is his normal homecoming time lately. He eats something and lies in bed reading until I go in and tell him to turn off his light and go to sleep. He just can't seem to go to bed by himself.
>
> Today he went to school at his insistence on six hours sleep. But he was worrying about being late because *that* is one of the few rules of this special summer school at Jr. High —the students must get there on time and regularly.
>
> I told him that starting tonight, the door will be locked by 11 P.M. on school night. If he can't make it home by then, he is on his own. I can't keep his hours. I hope this is not a mistake.
>
> Day after day, night after night, Mike is "away"—disappearing on a motorcycle or in a car (never the same com-

panions for more than two weeks) in whatever reality he has found.

These boys seem all of a kind—pleasant enough, although non-committal; moving unsmilingly like robots, beings from another planet. There is no communicating with them, but I suspect they are much different away from grown-ups.

It is impossible to talk to Mike, although I have tried to be matter-of-fact in approaching him. His eyes show he isn't even in the house. I just don't recognize this boy any more. He is so detached, remote, mechanical and strange. He is pleasant, seldom flares up at me—I'm not important enough to him for anger. When he walks in at 1 A.M. nightly he always says carelessly and without feeling, "Sorry I'm late, Mom." However, the night he got in at 2 A.M., he went downstairs for milk, noticed the time and came into my room with a shaking voice to say, "Gosh, Mom, I really had no idea it was so late." Once in a while reality touches his world and frightens him.

My authority is nil. He doesn't dispute it; just doesn't even notice it. I don't know if he uses drugs. He shows no physical signs of it except this other-world remoteness, which may just be his "time" difficulties. One night, in a rare conversation, he sat with me for 1½ hours telling me about the seriousness of the drug problem in our town. He spoke maturely and with such knowledge of the situation that I was frightened (for the sake of such a young person admitting that he has *never* gone downtown without being approached by a dealer!). He knows *everything* about drugs. Get him to tell you about it sometime. Also, he seemed genuinely concerned about the drug scene and his friends' involvement in it.

The girls used to call him constantly. Now, perhaps because he is never at home, the phone seldom rings for him. Even his contact system has moved outside the house.

I really don't know where Mike is going, but he's picking up speed. He keeps saying he knows what he is doing, that I have no idea of the life he leads. But he seems unable to tell me about it.

He seems so hopeless and miserable in one way, and so uncaring in another.

In those desperate early-morning hours, when it's hard to believe in possibilities, I have thought of several things. Would he wear one of those love bead bells around his neck as a reminder to check on the time? (He's willing to try.) A watch with an alarm? (I know he'd lose it.) Hypnotism—I'm serious

—maybe he could be hypnotized to think of checking the time when he sees or hears something on his person.

Do you think he would accept a foster home? I feel sure he would run away or just waste away. And maybe that would be the final rejection, since he must know he is unacceptable in behavior. I sense that he needs support and help desperately. And at the same time he seems so sure of himself and what he is doing; as if it's all planned. He says he would like to be a counselor because "you can't learn to help people by taking courses in college but by being out there with the winos and the guys in trouble." He is always very perceptive.

Even his efforts to fit in are so pathetic. Like getting a bath and hair-wash at 3:30 A.M. and, when I inquired what he was doing, replying in surprise, "But you *said* to get a bath tonight, Mom."

I think he has found some sort of world for himself, and God knows he has lots of company in it. But it's a here-and-now world with no yesterday and no tomorrow, as you know so well. The barber was saying yesterday that he runs into Mike all over town—"Such a friendly boy." He's all over town, all right, but I admit I feel guilty, as if I were avoiding taking steps to put him in some sort of situation with limits.

Perhaps he must find his own way with no help. But then, why am I here?

One thing—nobody will accept the fact that he really and truly has no concept of time. My best friends think I'm just being too lax. Nonsense. Everyone can be taught to operate on schedule. He's pulling the wool over my eyes, they're sure.

If you get any ideas, pass them on. Meanwhile I shall try belling my stray cat in the hope of reminding him he has a home.

                                                          Sincerely,
                                                          Mike's mother

What Happens to Them Later?

It's important to understand these kids because they are the ones that become the marginally adjusted, the frequenters of Mental Health Centers. This doesn't have to be because many also become leaders of men—

> doctors
> lawyers
> accountants
> salesmen
> presidents

As they grow older, they disappear—not all, but most. Some, some, who were "one of those kids" become very successful. They who were so totally disorganized, become totally organized—slaves to time and sequence—and the slavery pays off in the job market though their families may experience regimentational discomfort.

It is as though the hopelessness of internal matching to external demands becomes the accepted mode and he becomes the unquestioning slave to clock and to superior others.

When you've spent a lifetime of puzzlement and questioning about being out of step—of failure when trying to determine your own beginnings and endings—of always asking the *why* which is obvious to all— you accept with relief the clock of the other and ask but blindly to follow tradition of teacher, of agency, of God. And you do it this way because that's the way it's done and method and order precede and eclipse meaning and situational requirements.

And the number of jobs open to slaves of tradition are multitudinous for superiors require subordinates. The tradition-bound subordinate is superior as the theory of ours not to question why but to do as programmed becomes the *modus operandi* of neatly dressed machines who don't even jump if you shout at them. The small clues that used to be so minutely and inappropriately attended to, defined one as hyperactive, are now ignored totally in the vast all or none.

Standards of accomplishment of judging self or others are measured by the yardsticks of rightness or wrongness dissociated totally from circumstance. "I understand, but . . ." becomes an automatic phrase as all impact follows the *but*.

And the slaves wear the masks of their masters and cherish their ticking though the clocks have all stopped. The fact that they're killing you is incidental if procedure is right and tradition preserved.

Form becomes the thing and you go through the motions. It's not what you do but how you are seen doing that gets you the goodies and power over others in the complex spy system of the unrocking boat. And lessons are learned too well for the neatly dressed and neatly numbered. They know when to holler at others and being good at math has paid off for *this* is the problem and you've not done it right.

How do these changes happen? What is their extent? From what to what?

From	To
Life and its events happen to me —I am not the initiator; I am simply here and in trouble. I see it, I want it, I take it. What's bad about that? Whataya mean I don't learn from experience— who experiences? What's experience? In accordance with *whose* needs?	Give me the recipe—you, there outside me—outline the steps toward a functioning life and I follow it blindly though no one eats cake. If the recipe is timed short—say, just for the work days—the evenings are rough and the weekends are worse—but when he's sober you couldn't ask for a nicer guy.
	The length of the cycle determines style and diagnosis—the instant motor tic—the speech block or repeat—to the total blanket of ritual religion or analysis.
	Automaticity becomes too well learned.

What happens to them later? Well. . . .

Are there connections between learning disability and alcoholism? It makes you wonder.

The mother of the disorganized child says:	The wife of the alcoholic says:
He's so irresponsible.	He's so irresponsible.
Sometimes you couldn't ask for a nicer kid.	When he's sober, you couldn't ask for a nicer guy.
He loves animals.	He gets along great with little kids and animals.
He says he's sorry but he messes up again.	His promises don't mean anything.
He blames others for his troubles —nothing is ever his fault.	He's always got an excuse.
Thinks only of himself.	Spends his whole paycheck.
Living with him is like walking on eggs.	You never know how he's going to be when he comes home at night.
I get so angry I'm ashamed of myself.	I'm angry most of the time.
He never seems to appreciate anything I do for him.	I try everything I know to please him, but it doesn't seem to make any difference.
He embarrasses me.	He embarrasses me—Is it my fault?
You can never tell; the least little thing can set him off, even if it's positive.	Anything can make him start drinking. If he gets in trouble at work, he gets drunk to celebrate, and if nothing happens, he gets drunk because he's bored!
At some things he works till he drops.	He'll work all day—on someone else's car.
He cons me all the time.	He cons me all the time.
He says he's going to change but it never lasts.	He promises me and I believe him. But I can never depend on him for sure.
He's a complete mess or he's perfect.	There's no in-between; he's all or nothing.

He gets everybody screaming at him.	I get so mad I scream at him and then I think it's my screaming that makes him the way he is.
He's smart enough he ought to be doing better.	Listen, he knows how to do things. It's like he can't stand success.
He's a good salesman.	He sells me a bill of goods all the time. I get mad at myself because I believe him.
It's terrible to feel such a failure as a mother.	It's terrible to feel such a failure as a wife.
I feel so sorry for him I could cry.	I feel so sorry for him I could cry.
I don't know what to do to help him.	I've tried everything and nothing works.
I give him a chance to do something nice, and he says, "No."	He didn't even come home for his own son's birthday party.

The parallel descriptions of disorganized children and alcoholics are striking. There are other parallels also: the ratio of male to female is about the same. They function best in structured situations. The literature contains little agreement as to cause and effect. They have a similar orientation toward time—seem to live only for the moment. Many children with learning disability have fathers who are or were practicing alcoholics. It is not unusual for the alcoholic to report difficulty in school—handwriting may still be very poor. Etiological descriptions are so varied that multiple causation is likely in both instances.

They don't *all* become alcoholics. Perhaps alcoholism is one way of adapting to the absence of a causative self. Certainly the "submission" to external controls and regulation is evident in many alcoholics who alternate between total disorganization and total organization—"obsessive compulsive" symptoms, and being chronically drunk.

There are some indications suggesting that the drugs of today substitute for the booze of yesterday.

It's not too much later for Pete. He's seventeen and has been referred to the Mental Health Center. Parents still get blamed, but at seventeen, he also becomes an acceptable target.

Pete has been referred by his mother. She is concerned because he seems to have no energy, no enthusiasm, and no desire to succeed in school or anything else.

He is awkward—could never achieve anything in athletics. He reads in his room and makes demands on her constantly for the car, money, and other things.

Pete has not graduated from high school because he did not turn in a final paper for the course he took in journalism. She describes him as always late; as keeping lists for everything. The lists become longer and longer as he does less and less. She says he was a slow-learner in school (measured intelligence is superior). His mother reports:

Pete was a passive boy, a good baby. I fed him until he was two years old because he didn't seem to want to do it for himself. He was slow to walk. This all changed at age five when he became excitable and upset and I had trouble controlling him. He was always on the move, restless. I had to watch him because I just didn't feel comfortable leaving him alone. He was so impulsive, plunged into things. He had to be first and didn't take turns even then. In school he was always a slow-learner and school seemed difficult for him. He always seemed bright enough, but somehow he didn't achieve. Everyone said he didn't work up to his capacity: he could if he wanted to, but he wouldn't apply himself. He was very irresponsible. He seemed not to have any real interest in anything. He would start things, but never follow through or complete them. I had to be on him all the time or he did nothing. He still accuses me of being on his back. Believe me, I don't want it to be that way. I'd be mighty happy if he could get going on his own. It just doesn't seem to work out that way. He doesn't seem to understand that there are consequences: if he does this, then that follows; or if he doesn't do this, then that follows. The same things happen over and over. He doesn't seem to learn from experience. Explanations don't help. And, apparently, his being smart doesn't help either.

He's different from my other children. If I did everything wrong with kids, how come the others aren't messed up? What worked for them didn't work with him. Nothing seemed to matter very much to him, at least not for very long. I punished him until I felt bad—I spanked him. He'd get over it, and it was like it never happened. He'd get awfully mad, and he still does, but he doesn't stay mad. He never seems to understand what I'm talking about—griping about. He doesn't feel sorry about anything; I wonder if I ever get through to him. He forgets things and he loses things . . . it's like he doesn't care. It sure doesn't seem important for him to please us. But he seems to feel justified in demanding that we please him. He asks for everything as if he had it coming to him, and doesn't seem to feel that he is under any obligation to do anything to earn things. He wants what he wants right now . . . and he wants so much. In some ways he seems very immature, and then again, if he's not wanting anything, so independent, as if he doesn't need anyone.

He seems to think that other people exist to serve him. And unless they are busy serving him, they shouldn't bother him. The whole family revolves around him—it's always been that way. He seems to feel that this is the way it should be and doesn't appreciate it. What is it with him, anyway? Is he emotionally disturbed? It doesn't seem to me that *he's* disturbed, but I am. It has to be something I've done wrong, and I feel guilty about it, but I really can't figure out what it is. I've tried everything I know to change the situation, but nothing works. There *is* a lot of turmoil in our family. My husband doesn't seem to be worried about him (as much as I am) and we disagree about him all the time. I don't think it is the turmoil that has made him the way he is. I think it is he that has caused the turmoil, but I don't know just how. He doesn't even look unhappy, but the rest of us do.

Pete was seen by the social worker who described him as a charming and cooperative boy. He did not display any signs of tension or anxiety although he did have some compulsive symptoms; he trimmed his fingernails even when they didn't need it, and picked lint off his socks. When asked about his mother he described her as being overly-critical and bossy and said he was at the Mental Health Center because she wanted him to come. He stated that there were no problems in his life that required the services of a Mental Health Center. This was a matter-of-fact statement. He would come if his mother wanted him to. He expressed himself well and his vocabulary suggested above-average intelligence. He really didn't say anything about himself. He refused to mention the impulsive kind of behavior that his mother described. He was unable to say what it was about him that bothered his mother so much. In talking about his mother he indicated that she was hard to please and gave as an example her telling him to be independent and then not approving of the idea he came up with to carry out this independence. It seemed to the social worker that Pete was presently immobilized, had no long-range plans, and seemed rather unconcerned about not having graduated from high school.

After talking with the parents it seemed important to get information about his functioning directly from the school staff. The principal was contacted and reported that Pete did not graduate because he did not get a paper in on time. He was enrolled in a course in journalism and the paper was due on May 29th, but it was not turned in. He had been told that if the paper was not turned in he would not graduate. And so, school officials were surprised when he appeared for the class picnic. "I told him he was not permitted to do this because he did not get the paper in. I expected him to be angry, but he wasn't. He accepted it. So then I figured he couldn't care less. I thought that he was probably hiding his feelings, but it didn't appear to be that way. The teacher gave him another chance, and extended the deadline to the middle of June. He handed in eight handwritten pages, double-spaced, when the assignment called for thirty typewritten pages, single-spaced." (Up to this point there was no indication that the school suspected he couldn't do this assignment. Rather, they seemed to feel that he could do it if he wanted to. He just didn't.) The principal then read a report written by the teacher who stated that the quantity of his work in her course had been poor throughout the entire semester, as had the quality. The principal concluded that the school should not have permitted him to take the course, but Pete expressed himself so well verbally it was hard to remember he couldn't put ideas in writing.

The principal felt Pete was bright enough because he had a high I.Q. on a group test. He noted that on achievement tests there was always a wide spread in scores. In general, intelligence and achievement tests indicated that he would be capable of doing A and B work. When questioned about Pete's attitude, the principal stated that he had always been polite, that there had never been any smart-talk. He described him as being a loner, as not having a single close friend in the year and a half he had attended that school. When asked if Pete seemed to be responsible the principal answered, "It depends upon what you're talking about. He did an excellent job selling ads for the Annual, but on another assignment, such as getting a paper done which had been assigned six weeks in advance, he didn't do well at all. Not only that; he didn't ask for help so we had no way of knowing that he was in trouble because he certainly isn't shy."

His strengths were working in areas where the job was specific and exact when there was only one way to do it.

The principal was very positive about Pete not having any sense of time. He lived only a short distance from school, but was frequently late. When he arrived late, he didn't go to class, but would walk, roaming the halls. The principal knew that the parents were worried about Pete and remembered they had expressed concern about whether or not he would graduate when Pete entered the school. He couldn't understand why the parents considered him a slow-learner, and said the only note in the cumulative record was one stating that Pete had been placed in advanced science in the ninth grade because of his high test scores. The principal said that if he had to say three things about Pete, he would say that he was a roamer, a loner, and always late. The principal felt they had worked very diligently with Pete, but somehow they just never got through to him.

From the mother's initial concern that Pete didn't finish high school, more problems were elaborated involving the whole family. The mother doesn't know how much longer she can go on being a mother to her other children or a wife to her husband if this boy remains in the home. She feels guilty that she wants "out" so much, but she has had it. And she gives you examples with periods and paragraphs how it has been through all his growing years:

It is Sunday morning. Everyone is ready to go to church. He announced earlier that he wanted to go with them. But he is still in bed. When they call, again, he comes downstairs in his bare feet, unshaven and still wearing his pajamas. They finally decide to leave without him, and he cannot understand why they refuse to wait.

Now it is vacation time, and he has ruined every vacation for the whole family for years. For example, they are on a trip and they stop He doesn't want to go with them and do what the others do. They agree to go separate ways and meet at the car at 3:30. They are waiting for him in the hot car at 3:30 and he shows up 45 minutes later, no apologies, and puzzled because they are mad.

We take the camper and enjoy it, but it means that everyone has a job to do, especially Pete, the oldest. Does he? No, he does not. He doubles everybody's work. The others insist that it isn't fair, and they wonder why we let him get away with it. I'm leveling the camper and driving stakes, his job, and he's griping at me because supper isn't ready. I decided that I would rather stay home than travel under these conditions. This year he is eighteen—maybe we could go on vacation and leave him at home. But do we dare? You'd think at eighteen he could take care of himself for a week. But it's not only taking care of himself that I'm worried about. What might happen to our house and the car? Not long ago he had strict instructions to leave the car in the garage when we were gone. When we got back, we learned that he had another key made and drove it all over town with his friends. He also forgot to turn off the fire on the stove, and he left water running to overflowing in the bathtub.

Pete was referred for psychological testing in hopes for some direction and clarification. A report was received:

Intelligence: Superior—(He has the knowledge to behave within societies norms if he should chose to do so.)

Vocabulary definitions indicate some formality and awkwardness of phrasing which is suggestive of obsessional thinking.

Superior functioning on the vocabulary and block design subtests would suggest there is no loss of abstract attitude apparent so that organicity in a general sense certainly is not present.

The lowest subtest of 8 suggests he was slow and left-handed which also suggests obsessive-compulsive defenses.

Benton designs were right at the norm for superior intelligence.

Rorschach failed to show most of those signs typically indicative of organic involvement. His Rorschach was somewhat diffuse; there were suggestions of paranoid thinking and generally not up to the performance expected on the basis of superior intelligence. This may indicate that in creative activity his intellectual efficiency is not up to his intellectual potential. Tendencies to ruminate over unnecessary details, to vascillate in decisions and to inhibit assertive responses could result in such intellectual inefficiency.

The MMPI code does not agree with the serious, ruminating intense person described above.

At any rate, the psychologist's conclusion was, "Organicity in the sense of loss of the abstract attitude is not present, and while the general impression (Rorschach) is of a bright person who has developed obsessive-compulsive behavior with low energy level, the MMPI is more suggestive of a very energetic person who could be expected to behave impulsively and come into friction with society's mores either through delinquent behavior or sexual acting out."

So—what happens to these children later? It's still happening to Pete. He's now nineteen, has been in and out of the home, in and out of a Day Treatment Program, and is receiving encouragement from his parents to join the service. He's collecting labels and people still say, "He could if he wanted to," and he agrees . . . for his existence depends on your definitions.

Remediation

Sensory integration is not a slowly developing phenomenon. It is a sudden "Ah-Ha"—a coming together, a great leap forward, a light bulb flashing in the head, the chill down the spine when you hear the stately measures, "Mine eyes have seen the Glory of the Coming of the Lord." It is Maslow's peak experience; Perl's "Lose your mind and come to your senses;" it is being-with; it is an orgasm of integration—the 'it' becomes 'I'—emanating from Kephart's center of gravity, not tacked on as a role.

And it is the lack of centeredness, lack of self-as-doer, the paucity of positive I-Did-Its, that makes integration impossible.

That's why the teachings of the nit-picking do not generalize, and generalization is a huge problem. That's why he doesn't remember. That's why his behavior and learnings are situational—the *sayin*'s and *doin*'s and *knowin*'s remain ever separate. The *I* that includes all-of-me is unconnected, unzipped, and sensory experience in one mode cannot be imaged in another. "There is no string for my beads so I take a few with me and spend most of my time trying not to drop the ones I have but doing so every time I reach for a new one." Self-awareness must and can be directly taught.

Functioning in the service of others, as directed by others, prevents development of a causative self; creates and sustains "learning disability" as do the parents who "blame themselves"—for if the parents take credit for shaping the child, causes remain outside the child and life continues to "happen to him."

The hundreds of negative "You did its" serve further to stop development of a causative self.

You can't get up and walk around without the muscle-bone connected to the ear-bone; the ear-bone connected to the eye-bone; the eye-bone connected to the muscle-bone . . .

> He can't hear if there is
> no one inside listening.
>
> He can't see if there is
> no one inside looking.

114

He can't remember if there
is no rhythm to interrupt.

He can't feel if there is
no one inside to hurt.

So,

he doesn't *put* himself in your place—he is always *in* your place kicking
hell out of you.

If there is no "I" to suffer, there is no regret, no guilt—no tomorrow,
no yesterday—no reason to think you suffer. *I* didn't do it because *I* do
not exist.

IT Happened.

"Hey, Mom. The bed wet me again!"

The denial of one's actions becomes denial of one's self for action and
self are not separated.

So he learns-by-doing, but the guts of the learning, the glue binding tomorrows, is the positive I—did it!

> The problem is doing things for him.
> It's OK to do things *with* him.

Got A Match?

The "appropriate" level of sensitivity is related to surroundings:

$$\frac{\text{SITUATIONAL DEMANDS}}{\text{INDIVIDUAL RESPONSE}} = \text{I}$$

$$\frac{\text{situational demands}}{\text{INDIVIDUAL RESPONSE}} = \text{get HIM!}$$

$$\frac{\text{SITUATIONAL DEMANDS}}{\text{individual response}} = \text{PAY ATTENTION}$$

$$\frac{\text{situational demands}}{\text{individual response}} = 1$$

$$\frac{\text{READ}}{\text{read}} = \text{dyslexia} \qquad \frac{\text{READ}}{\text{READ}} = \text{A}$$

$$\frac{\text{read}}{\text{READ}} = \text{don't teach him at home} \qquad \frac{\text{read}}{\text{read}} = \text{slow track}$$

$$\frac{\text{SPELL}}{\text{spel}} = \text{F}$$

Accordance among persons of similar levels of awareness is more tuneful. This accounts for fathers seeing problems less looming. (If fathers taught school, boy referrals would slow.)

Major matching attempts at home and in schools are between mothers and children; school marms and kids. The females are active—they do all the teaching. The task of reception is the student-borne load.

To receive or learn without action is difficult for most and impossible for some. The reaching for knowledge, the active grabbing toward goals, occurs most frequently among boys. (Even as infants, reaction time is faster—later interpreted as "poor impulse control!") And it is least tolerated by females who require less impact to pattern and flow.

Tolerance varies among teachers (he makes it with one and not with another), but the average sensitivity level is above the average for males. The range of general teacher-tolerance includes all but nine percent— eight boys and one girl. (If you don't fit you get referred to get re-fitted.)

Integration is matching, marching harmony. Most focus so far has been on the inside organs of relationship each to each, their imbalance seen jagged or heard noisy. But the insides can be too perfectly balanced as in the hypoactive child—in step with self but not with others or situations. He's got two speeds, slow and stopped, and seldom can move with the group.

The match between teacher demand and student response is easier to maintain in a one-to-one situation. "When I have him by himself he can do it," is an observation frequently made.

The situation is further complicated by the demands of curriculum imposed on the teacher. Teacher expectations based on curriculum are often not realistic for a particular child. The complications generated by having to cover too much material sometimes leads to further exclusion of children in the learning process. Curricula demanding maximum activity of the teacher, rushing to cover prescribed material within prescribed time, will miss many children. It's like teaching singing using a dog whistle for a pitch pipe. For children tuned lower, the task is impossible, but the teaching has been done, they just didn't learn.

Children do better if actively involved in the process; they assume reaching roles when there is a demand-response match. Classrooms organized around doing-in-space with children active, produces fewer mis-fits than classrooms organized in time units with children passive. The child reaches out and does at an activity level, chosen by self, to fit his own needs. That's why the observation, "THEY BECOME THEIR OWN BEST THERAPIST" *if* you provide a situation allowing greater intensity and extensity of impact, child-chosen on the basis of need.

Ouch!

He woke up screaming in the middle of the night. He had a temperature—I thought related to the chicken pox and measles which he had suffered recently in combination. This was the first indication that something was seriously wrong. My experience with him was if he hollered he really hurt. I was scared when I called the doctor. I was panicked. I rushed to the emergency room at the hospital. It took a nurse and two attendants to hold Brian, just to be examined. I stayed in the room helpless and useless and scared. The doctor said Brian had a severe ear infection. It would be necessary to lance the eardrum. They immobilized him for the delicate surgical procedure. His screaming and thrashing put everyone on edge. The doctor barked at me, "This didn't just happen. He's been in pain for days." His accusation was echoed by a quick frown from the nurse and the two attendants. The message was clear. I failed him again. I was a terrible mother. I left the room. I felt guilty about that, too. They didn't need me to help, but leaving. . . . I really couldn't stand it. His pain and my guilt were too much. Not the time to explain, but, I had *not* neglected this child. So help me, I didn't even know he was hurting!

The doctor didn't believe how advanced the strep infection was when he looked at her throat. It was practically closed. And her complaints were still minor. That's nothing—her little finger was broken for two days before the swelling brought it to her attention. She showed it to me as a curiosity. It was larger than it should be. She finally remembered that it was bent way back when it was hit by a ball. X-rays showed it to be broken.

Spanking does no good. He doesn't even cry unless I half kill him. I'm afraid to hit him. He says, "Go ahead, you have to pay the hospital bill." I get so angry. There must be something terribly wrong with me.

There's something different about him. He can be outside playing and break his arm or get a severe cut that's bleeding, requires stitches, and he doesn't come in until he is through playing.

He comes in with a stinger of a bee sticking out of the swelling in his finger, and says, "A bee stung me." My other children would come in screaming for me to put something on it. The stinger was a curiosity. He wanted to show me. He pulled it out and went on.

She opened the back car door and fell out when it was moving, was skinned from head to foot. She looked terrible. She didn't even cry until they separated her from me in the emergency room. She doesn't cry from physical pain. Why?

The above examples show the differences between these children and other children to be more extensive than inability to read, write, spell or figure. Still, most remedial prescriptions take the form of "teaching an academic skill to bring them up to grade level." This difference in sensitivity, for example, has personality consequences beyond academics. He hits other children too hard. He hits harder—he assumes others require impact of matching intensity for the hit to register.

This physical unawareness of self, in comparison with others, extends to include awareness of self in space (he must touch and bump to know where he is); awareness of self as "cause" ("I didn't hit him hard—I just tapped him."); awareness of self as existing in time (he's so busy impacting, experiencing self

yesterday   NOW   tomorrow

Intention doesn't match reactions of others. He's puzzled by assumptions others make concerning motive (they exaggerate so!).

It is easy for him to see how it is between others. He assumes each external other experiences like him, at his impact level, so perception is matched each to each. (He is quick to blame others, never seeing his part.) He denies his role as initiator, "I didn't do it," for he participates at a different level of awareness. There is no response to gentle physical impact or subtle nuances. He's all or none.

Insensitivity affects other's perception of parents: "This didn't just happen—there's been pain for days!"

—parent's perception of child: "He makes me look bad as a mother."

—teacher's view of him: "He's unaware that he makes himself unpopular."

—child's perception of parent: "What you so upset about? I'm OK."

—and on in interpersonal reverberations—to the labels which stem from other's awareness of his unawareness. "If I, at my awareness level, behaved in this situation as he does, I would call myself,

> mean
> a bully
> thickskinned
> selfish
> snoopy
> a braggart
> a liar
> smart-mouthed
> a pest
> a con-artist
> a loner
> lazy
> a trouble-maker
> careless
> messy
> pushy
> a poor loser
> a cheater
> a thief
> a clown
> bossy
> demanding
> irresponsible
> a nuisance,

for I assume his awareness-range approximates mine."

And labels are pasted attempts to glue the mismatched together.

Pills

We are not physicians. We do not know the long-range effects of medication. We are aware that this is a controversial procedure. We are also aware of many positive reports made by parents and teachers after a child is placed on stimulant drugs prescribed by his family physician or by a psychiatrist. Our observations indicate that the drugs increase body awareness and sensitivity, thus decreasing the need for stimulation gained by movement and seeking behavior. We feel that there are ways to increase sensitivity and awareness by means other than stimulant drugs, but the drugs seem to have a more immediate and dramatic effect.

With *this* child—we don't need your counseling. (They were talking about their changed boy.) Two weeks before they were begging for help with their son whose problems extended back to moment of birth and maybe before—he was hyperactive in the womb!

> He goes to his room—and does things—by himself. He's still up at 6:30, but he's not at us. He turns on his radio, softly, and reads—comes downstairs at 7:45 ready to go to school!
>
> He doesn't wander off. He says, "If you want me, just ring the bell—or better still, I'll come in to check,"—and he *does*!
>
> He fiddles with old radios—we have a lot—he grounded the lead wire, burned his hand. He *felt* it, he knew that he did it—that it didn't just happen. He even cleaned the black smudge off the wall.
>
> He still talks quite a bit, but he can stick to the subject.
>
> I don't have to say no all the time because he's not asking all the time. It's *easy* to give to him now—it's like it's my choice.
>
> It's more than just being able to tolerate and live with him—we enjoy him. We don't ask inside anymore, "Will he ever amount to anything?" It doesn't seem so pressing, so necessary

that we do something to change him. He looks different—he *is* different. He's doing for self—it's not *all* up to us.

For the first time in his entire life he went to the store with his 25¢ allowance—and came back with a dime! !

He says, "The medicine makes me hear better." I don't know if he hears better or not—but he sure seems to understand better.

One change is hard to describe—he was always at the car, demanding, when I came home. Once, I got mad—said, "Couldn't you at least ask how I feel or find out my mood or say 'Hi' before draining me dry?" The next night he met me: "Hi dad, how you feel. I found me a set of drums for you to buy." He said, "Hi, how you feel," but didn't *mean* it. Well, that's kinda how it's different. It's like he means what he says now—like he cares about us more—can sense our mood, can adjust his demands. He's more sensitive—he fits better.

How can two little pills twice a day make such a difference?? He's been upset for nine years. Things still happen, but not all the time. Like this morning he bumped the leg on the kitchen table and it collapsed. He clenched his fists to his sides and his whole body tensed like I was going to hit him. Ordinarily we would all have been in orbit, but I knew the leg was loose—I really wasn't mad—I started picking up dishes, asked him to help, and we both laughed! If it isn't *all* the time, you *can* laugh.

Listen, the whole neighborhood has noticed the change in Bobby, and three mothers wonder if there's help for their kids.

Bobby reports that his teacher and mother have both changed a lot since he started taking his pills.

When Bobby was first seen he sat on the edge of his chair, thin, dark and restless, and when asked, "What kind of problems do you have?" he twisted his buttocks to the left and his neck to the right, lifted his hands toward heaven, rolled his eyes, and said, "I don't knoooow—I'm naughty. I'm there, and all of a sudden I'm naughty. I don't know why . . . it just happens."

Bobby was started on a low dosage of medication with questionable results. His physician, instead of discontinuing the medication, increased the dosage. His mother marvels. "We didn't know it could be so nice." Bobby's mother reports that she is happy when he gets off the school bus in the afternoon . . . since he started on the medication. Not only that; he gets dressed and catches the school bus in the morning on time. He is able to relate and share more appropriately.

"I dunno—it just happened."

Bobby was a bed-wetter and a very hyperactive boy whose previous physician suggested that he should run around the block several times each morning before he went to school. The circles under his eyes got darker, he became more hyperactive, and bed-wetting increased. The parents purchased a bell-ringing pad which went off with loud, clanging noises two or three times each night, awakening everyone in the house except Robert. They stopped using the pad for none slept except him.

Bed-wetting frequency was cut in half even on the low dosage of medication. Now, it doesn't occur at all.

The mother accounted for Robert's difficulties as being related to the fact that they were a military family and Robert had changed schools several times during his ten years. She stated, however, that her daughter was a pleasant, cooperative girl who seemed unaffected by these moves. And her conclusion was, "I just don't know how to raise boys."

Melvin's parents reported that he was extremely fidgety:

    always moving
    can't sit still
    no power of concentration
    fights continuously
    has no respect for authority

is not working up to his capacity in school
made all Fs on his last report card
does anything to get attention
likes success and hates failure

On Saturday he began taking medication twice a day. On Tuesday the teacher reported:

What happened to Melvin?!?!
Seems like a completely new person.
He can sit still!
His feet haven't been on his desk for two days.
In reading circle he hasn't dropped his book once and he doesn't lose his place.
His writing is neater and he keeps at it longer.
He came up to me and talked to me about things that interested him. He never did that before!
He has responded to invitations from other children to join them in play and activities. They involve him, and he becomes involved.

Pamela's speech when she first gets up in the morning is unintelligible until fifteen-twenty minutes after taking her first twenty mgms of medication. (Pamela, now in the fifth grade, had been in speech therapy since kindergarten with only slight improvement.)

Few physician's feel comfortable prescribing for these children. This is based on fears related to drug abuse in adolescence or the fact that in the 1 to 1 situation in the physician's office disorganization is minimal. The physician believes reports of parents and teachers are exaggerated. The fact that hyperactivity is situational sometimes leads to the assumption that the difficulty is the result of an overanxious mother.

Medication, to be effective, requires time, adjustment of dosage, and sometimes different medication or a combination. Often parents are given too much responsibility in monitoring medication, and, just as often, not enough.

One of the reasons leading to the discontinuation of medication stems from the priority given to the school's complaints about the child. Parents figure that the child is somehow their fault, so they complain less vigorously about their difficulties with him. In the majority of cases medication is prescribed to extend only through the school day. When he gets home in the late afternoon the parents experience little change and sometimes give up medication if communication with the school is not open.

"The Doctor says it's just a phase. He'll outgrow it in 7 years when he's 12."

There are many physicians who tell parents, "He'll outgrow it." And he will, usually, when he hits adolescence—at least the need for medication will no longer exist. But, during the crucial years, between five and twelve, he experiences negative labeling that leaves life-long scars.

Sensory awareness can be increased with medication. Increased sensory awareness leads to emergence of causative self—that positive separateness that allows going back, being with, and viewing forward.

In Search of I

There is confusion and disagreement concerning how and why medication works. The idea that "stimulants" have an "opposite effect" on "these kids" is not valid. They have an organizing effect, resulting in increased sensitivity and awareness of self and environment.

These children are variously described as having a "high pain threshold," of being unaware of their impact on others and of disregarding attempts to structure and focus them.

Medication increases body sensitivity and body awareness just as it does when taken by a "normal" person. The difference is that medication takes the "normal" person *beyond* the point of organization while it takes "these kids" *up to* the point of organization and awareness.

It takes *less* impact to make an impression with increased awareness, and the child bangs up against his environment *less* vigorously—both physically and psychologically.

Hyperactivity is a stimulus seeking, motoric attempt to make contact, for it is through contact and bumping against that we know we are separate from the environment and others, to know we exist. For most of us, the air pressure on us outlines the self. For these children it does not. Only body surface in direct contact with objects means "me-ness." If you sit at a desk the awareness of feet on floor and butt on chair form a two dimensional and disconnected perception of self. You must move around and touch and make contact, or you cease to exist. For many, lying on the floor, with as much contact as possible, gives maximum feeling of self, or constant movement against air pressure (rocking for some; for others any motion) gives more feeling of existence. No wonder they sleep in a coma, no wonder bladder signals can't cut through. It's *not* true that they never get tired—they do, as they desperately search for the whole self.

That's why being in water is "fun."

That's why they respond negatively when barometric pressure falls. (He's worse when the weather is bad.)

That's why there is a positive correlation between barometric pressure and duration of crying in infants.

That's why they like tight clothing—why he won't take his coat off.
That's why they become "tight" and "obsessive-compulsive."
That's why he reads better with your arms around him.
And that's why—for some—at the onset of adolescence, the increase in juices, hormones, desire, body awareness increases and the desperate search for self ends.